# Discovering The Borders I

## Other titles in this series

*Already published:*
Coghill: Discovering the Water of Leith
Crumley: Discovering the Pentland Hills
Freethy: Discovering Cheshire
Freethy: Discovering Coastal Lancashire
Freethy: Discovering Coastal Yorkshire
Freethy: Discovering Cumbria
Freethy: Discovering Dartmoor and South Devon
Freethy: Discovering Exmoor and North Devon
Freethy: Discovering Inland Lancashire
Freethy: Discovering Inland Yorkshire
Freethy: Discovering the Yorkshire Dales
Gemmell: Discovering Arran
Green: Discovering Hadrian's Wall
Henderson: Discovering Angus & The Mearns
Hendrie: Discovering West Lothian
Lamont-Brown: Discovering Fife
Maclean: Discovering Inverness-shire
Macleod: Discovering Galloway
Macleod: Discovering the River Clyde
Murray: Discovering Dumfriesshire
Orr: Discovering Argyll, Mull and Iona
Shaw Grant: Discovering Lewis & Harris
Simpson: Discovering Banff, Moray & Nairn
Smith: Discovering Aberdeenshire
Strawhorn and Andrew: Discovering Ayrshire
Thompson: Discovering Speyside
I. & K. Whyte: Discovering East Lothian
Willis: Discovering the Black Isle
Withers: Discovering the Cotswolds

# Discovering
# The Borders I

ALAN SPENCE

JOHN DONALD PUBLISHERS LTD
EDINBURGH

© Alan Spence 1992

All rights reserved. No part of this publication may
be reproduced in any form or by any means without
the prior permission of the publishers,
John Donald Publishers Ltd,
138 St Stephen Street, Edinburgh EH3 5AA.

ISBN 0 85976 360 9


*British Library Cataloguing in Publication Data*
A catalogue record for this book is available from
the British Library.

Phototypeset by The Midlands Book Typesetting Company,
Loughborough.
Printed & bound in Great Britain by J. W. Arrowsmith Ltd., Bristol.

# Introduction

Originally this book was intended to cover the entire Border Country, defined in this instance as the area administered by the Borders Regional Council. Attempting to take a geographical course from place to place, unusually as I live there, starting at the coast which was much easier to deal with in the winter months when writing commenced. With such a wealth of information it became apparent that by the time the line of the A 68 was reached the manuscript had already overrun the publishers limitation, hence this is 'Discovering The Borders I,' II will follow in due course.

This is the story of the eastern part of the Border country, historic and modern, factual and legendary. It has been impossible to mention every village, or recount every story associated with what was approximately the old counties of Berwick and Roxburgh. Nor has it been possible to attend every local festival and gala day. I have however over the past nine months visited most of the places mentioned in the text, others sometime within recent years. A confession must be made that time could not be found to visit the Mutiny Stones in the Lammermuirs or fit in a visit to Ferniehirst Castle during the limited opening hours there.

What my ramblings have confirmed is that the Borders is the most beautiful part of Britain, Borderers the most helpful and warm hearted of its people. My hope is that those reading the following pages shall get as much enjoyment from doing so as I had collecting information and photographs.

## *Dedication*

To the memory of my late great aunt Janet Goodfellow, who even in her many years furth from this land was always at heart a Borderer.

# Acknowledgements

My sincere thanks to all who have responded to my enquiries when compiling this book. Some are only voices at the end of a telephone line who have been most helpful in my blundering attempts at interviewing.

Among the official bodies who have provided information are:-
Borders Regional Council Planning Department.
Roxburgh District Council.
Ettrick and Lauderdale District Council.
Borders Development Agency.

My thanks to Douglas Gibson of Coldstream one time proprietor of G. W. Gibson who provided pics of Gipsy Coronation and the Tweed during the 1948 flood. Dave Smith of the Photo Centre, Berwick for Jim Clark and Berwick Rangers pics and the John Wood Gallery for the old Coldingham and St Abbs Head pic. Also Thomas Litster of Peebles for their usual immaculate b & w printing.

1992                                                              A.S.

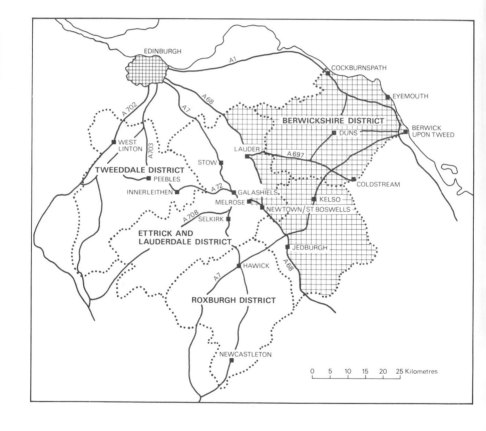

Location Map

# Contents

| | *Page* |
|---|---|
| Introduction | v |
| 1. The Place and the People | 1 |
| 2. Coastal | 25 |
| 3. The Merse | 56 |
| 4. Berwick on Tweed – The Scottish Connection | 103 |
| 5. Kelso to St Boswells | 117 |
| 6. St Boswells to Melrose | 145 |
| 7. Lauderdale | 163 |
| Further Reading | 175 |
| Index | 177 |

# CHAPTER 1

## *The Place and the People*

Writers on The Borders frequently quote from the works of Sir Walter Scott as an introduction to their work. A few lines from the man who was arguably the most famous Borderer of all time helps set the scene, or emphasises a point being made in the text. Quotations from Scott will no doubt feature in this book but the first cited work comes from elsewhere.

> When I die bury me low,
> Where I might hear the bonny Tweed Flow,
> A sweeter land I never did know,
> Than the rolling hills o the Border.

The above is the chorus to, 'The Rolling Hills O the Border' by the late Glasgow folk singer and song writer Matt Magin, set to the tune of the 'Soft Lowland Tongue of the Border.' Many of Matt's songs centred on the working life of Clydeside, or were humorous with an anti-Establishment message in their lines. Yet when Matt wrote these words he reflected the Borderers' feelings towards their native land. Of course the first human inhabitants, the hunter fishermen who had penetrated upstream alongside the Tweed after the retreat of the last Ice Age in 7000 BC would not have thought of themselves as Borderers. Mesolithic hunter/ fishermen/ gatherers were replaced by Neolithic Man who brought the first man-made changes to the landscape clearing parts of the native woodland for cultivation and pasturage. Little evidence remains of these early people other than their stone tools and weapons, some dating from 6000 BC.

Bronze Age dwellers left their mark throughout the Borders in burial chambers and stone circles, the former occasionally revealed by the plough to this day. Some idea of how many of these burial sites have been destroyed by cultivation can be gauged by the fact that where 14 once existed on the slopes of Linton Hill in Roxburghshire only one now remains.

1

The rolling Cheviots near Yetholm

The comment by the farmer who ploughed through the others sometime late in the nineteenth century being that the cairns only contained, 'a wheen rubbishy pots of earthenware'. Important finds from the Bronze Age in the shape of shields and axes have also came from Linton and Yetholm.

The culture of the Iron Age Celts who were something of displaced persons migrating north before the expanding Roman Empire, overtook that of the Bronze Age natives sometime around 500 BC. We have more evidence in the shape of their hill forts and camps above the contour line of modern cultivation; any settlements around this period on low ground must have long ago fallen to the plough. Notwithstanding any climatic differences there may have been then, it seems inconceivable that the Iron Age tribes would choose to live only in the upland areas. One thing that springs to mind when many of the Iron Age sites are visited is the lack of water. Was the first essential requirement for human existence all carried from the streams below or did these people of the Ottandi and further west the Selgovae tribes know the technology of well construction?

2

More than any other early invaders the Romans with their roads and military camps have left evidence on and below the ground for historians to ponder. Tribes of the Iron Age continued to occupy the Borders, before during and after the Roman occupation, whereafter the main influence came from the invasion of Germanic Angles who pushed the Celtic natives further and further back into the headwaters of the river valleys.

The Anglo-Saxon invasion and settlement was a gradual process, bringing in its wake improvements in agriculture. Christianity expanded with the Angles although little remains of their churches other than the sites, some of which have upon them places of worship still in use today. Anglian place names with 'ham' or 'wick' endings, as in Coldingham and Berwick, remain as evidence of their arrival and passing.

On the coast the Norse influence can still be found in the 'carr' and 'ness' description of coastal features — an influence reflected in the surnames of the coastal towns ending in 'son'; many of the bearers to this day are blue eyed and blond.

As sixth son of Malcolm III David I must have had little thought of ever bearing the Scottish crown. David had in fact spent much of his early life in England and on the Continent. It was King David who introduced into Scotland and the Borders the fuedal system along with the Norman families whose allegiance he had secured. A fair old mix of creeds and cultures are the Borders, and Borderers without a shadow of a doubt.

Mentioning The Borders to most people will focus their attention around the Scott Country, the mill towns of the middle Tweed, Ettrick and the Teviot. Yet the people of what was once the Eastern and part of the Middle March, approximately the old counties of Berwickshire and Roxburghshire, are equally proud of their heritage as the descendants of the riever clans of Teviot and Liddesdale.

For centuries the Marches of Scotland and England felt the hot breath of war upon their doorsteps, in peacetime the breath still fiery in theft and pillage. Only in 1603 when King James VI went south to become monarch of a United Kingdom, did a normal way of life such as had been enjoyed elsewhere within the two countries apply also to the Borderer. Peaceful periods between the nations did exist. Despite the impression often given that the nations of Scotland and England were perpetually at war with each other for five hundred years, there were times when at least the rulers were on friendlier terms. Some examples of short-term treaties include one agreed at Billy-Mire in 1386 between the earls of March and Douglas on the one hand and Lord Neville, Warden of the English East March. Terms for this included provision for each country to deal with rebels and enemies of the other. States of truce which were not necessarily appreciated by all dwellers on the frontier, who were of an independent mind when it came to deciding when and with whom they should be at odds.

Some of the deprivations suffered in Merse and Teviotdale can be judged by the years 1544 and 1545 during Henry VIII's rough wooing of Scotland. Evers, Layton and Bowes in 1544 having seized and fortified Coldingham Priory left this with an English garrison. Their further perambulations through the Merse and Teviotdale resulted in the destruction of 192 towns, towers and churches, 400 Scots slain, 800 taken prisoner and thousands of livestock stolen. Evers and Layton were jubilant, visiting the English court to boast that the Merse and Teviotdale were all but under English rule.

Messrs Evers and Layton got their come uppance at Ancrum Moor, being among the 800 English killed there, along with 2,000 taken prisoner who the Scots are said to have treated most barbarously, which is not surprising considering the devastation recently wrought upon the eastern March by the invaders.

Despite the destruction of 1544, Hertford was back the following year. Amazingly there was something left to burn, including in this case Coldingham, Kelso, Duns and Eccles, the towers of Nisbet, Redbraes, Mersington and Pollard, plus the castles of Wedderburn and Blackadder. Not exactly a pastoral scene of peace and ploughmen, the bounty of the fertile land difficult to sow, never mind reap.

Into this chaos came the Wardens, appointed by their respective kings to bring order among their own. Attempting to curb when required, the activities of their sovereign's subjects from upsetting those on the other side of the Cheviot range or river Tweed. The Warden system divided the Border into three sections, the East, Middle and West Marches, with Scottish and

English wardens appointed to each March. Wardens were, in theory at least, the king's representatives in the Borders, a policeman, judge, lawyer, diplomat, spy, a leader of forces and a loyal servant to the Crown. Not an easy task even in civilised times, and these were far from civilised times. The Home family were traditional Wardens of the East March where they seem to have had some degree of success in keeping order within their territory. The Kerrs of Cessford and Ferniherst, two branches of the same family which did not always see eye to eye with each other, were usually one or other Wardens of the Middle March.

A complicated set of laws, *Leges Marchairum*, was supposed to assist the wardens in settling cross-Border differences, meeting their opposite numbers at appointed places of truce on specific days. At these meetings a complaint from, for example, a Scot, who had been the victim of some offence perpetrated by someone from the English side, would have brought this matter to the notice of his own Warden. He in turn would raise the matter with his English counterpart on the day of truce, who in turn was duty bound to investigate and obtain some redress for the aggrieved. Briefly that was the system before the foibles of human nature were taken into account, personal opinion, family ties or even blatant self interest. Truce days, as will be seen later, could erupt into very warlike occasions. Remembering that in some places under discussion here there was an active reiving tradition, where the participants at least saw it as a normal way of life and not in any way a criminal activity.

Eventually the old March areas became Berwickshire and Roxburghshire, later to be replaced as Districts within the Borders Region, although the District boundaries do not exactly match those of the old counties. At the same time the Burgh status with its dignity of provost and council was removed from Border towns which held this right, as Royal burghs, police burghs or Burghs of Barony. This was deeply felt as here local civic pride is perhaps stronger than elsewhere in Scotland.

Upon the creation of the Borders Region the village of Newton St Boswells was a diplomatic choice for the new body's headquarters situated in the old Roxburgh District Council offices. Rivalry between the major towns, some with Royal

Burgh status, ensured that the selection of any one would be felt as an insult to the remainder. Parliamentary constituencies have changed, making a new seat of Roxburgh and Berwick, which is the nearest matching official designation of the area covered in this book with some exceptions where the text necessitates crossing lines drawn upon maps. It is approximately half the territory falling under the jurisdiction of the Borders Regional Council, yet it would be futile to talk or write of this part of the world in a historic or current sense without including Berwick on Tweed, an English town bearing the same name as a Scottish county, whose history and that of the Borders and Scotland have been long entwined.

Throughout the entire Borders Region the population stands at some 103,000 or 2 per cent of the Scottish total, where the main centres of population are the towns of Hawick and Galashiels. Politically it is Liberal Country, Archie Kirkwood having held the Roxburgh and Berwickshire seat since its creation.

Up country Sir David Steel is as much part and parcel of the Borders scene as the reiver's tower he is currently restoring, courtesy of a national newspaper which was foolish enough to libel the man who entered Parliament in 1966 as 'Boy David' the youngest member in the House. At Berwick on Tweed the seat there and Liberal MP Alan Beith seem inseparable. What, one wonders, do political analysts make of this triple enclave within the Borders? Ignoring administrative qualifications, this tract of land has fairly well-defined physical boundaries. Nothing is more definite than the precipitous Berwickshire coast; where cliff scenery is concerned it is something of an irony that this lowland agricultural county should boast some of the best seascapes in Britain.

Along the crest of the Lammermuirs, old roads used by inland monks still wend towards the fishing town of Dunbar in East Lothian. Down into Lauderdale, a natural highway since time immemorial, even before the Roman Legions established a camp at Kirktonhill below Turf Law where the last section of Dere Street climbs to the Lothian watershed. Through Lauderdale, past Earlston with its ruined Rhymers Tower, passing near the Abbeys of Dryburgh and Melrose where Eildons' three peaks have watched the march of Scottish history along the dale below. Jedburgh — another abbey — to the Carter Bar — a 'new' road replacing Redeswire Border crossing.

Then along the Cheviot's watershed, following the route of the Pennine Way over Beefstand Hill and Windy Gyle, Russel's Cairn marks the spot where an English representative at a truce day was mysteriously shot. On to Auchope Cairn on Cheviot above the Hen Hole gorge, then down over the Border Ridge to Yetholm and back to farming country. Here the trend is north-west to where the Tweed becomes the Border at Redden Burn.

Downstream past Birgham, Carham and Wark, tiny villages which all played a part in the making of Scotland and the establishment of the present Border. Coldstream down to Ladykirk and Norham where a few miles farther on the Border leaves Tweed to head almost due north to Clappers near Mordington. Continuing along the Liberty of Berwick, crossing the A1, where once stood a toll and marriage house as famous as Gretna Green, to rejoin the sea a few miles north of Berwick on Tweed at Lamberton.

Where this book is concerned the circuit described in the foregoing paragraphs is the area to be covered with some deviations. Within are once Royal Castles, the great Abbeys founded by David I of Scotland, 'the sair saint tae the croon'. Here are found the sites of battles, some famous — some obscure. Kings were born, died, crowned and by choice were buried here. A land where early Christian religion prospered, but a land where also dark deeds, battles and murder shaped the destiny of nations.

Here are found houses and estates, property of families whose origins date back to Anglian and Norman founders. Families who have figured boldly in the history of the Borders whose influence continues to the present day. Here once armed bands led by the forebears of one such family, after loosing the Wardenship to a foreigner, pursued the incumbent to final slaughter followed by the grisly public display of the unfortunate knight's head in open defiance. Or in disagreement with the royal selection of courtiers, took direct action by hanging these unfortunate favourites from the nearest bridge.

Battles there certainly were throughout the centuries where

the histories of both Scotland and England were influenced by victory or defeat. In major battles the Scots seemed to have come off second best with tragic defeats at Halidon Hill in 1333 and Flodden in 1513. Lesser bouts with English forces occurred with relentless regularity, invaders seeking not always to conquer, but to exact retribution for previous incursions south by the March men.

Like the incident in 1558 when Henry Percy, brother of the Duke of Northumberland, and Sir George Bowes Marshal of Berwick, with 700 horse and 2,000 foot, devastated part of the Merse as far as Langton and Duns. Returning with their booty a Scottish force intercepted them at Swinton where the Scots received a trouncing, this despite the fact that the English gunpowder failed to ignite due to the damp air of the Merse bogs.

Sedimentary rocks form the underlying strata throughout the Borders comprising Lower and Upper Red Sandstones and Carboniferous deposits. Upland areas share these under-lying rocks, the Lammermuirs dividing Berwickshire from the Lothians comprise tightly folded layers of Ordovican and Silurian Rocks of the Upper Old Red Sandstone age.

The Cheviots on the southern boundary, on the other hand, are the result of violent volcanic activity; below the soggy peat blanket lie granite rocks varying from pale buff to pink in colour. Throughout the Borders there are other evidences of a volcanic past; the triple peaks of the Eildon Hills are composed of volcanic rock but are not volcanoes, being the most outstanding examples.

Like other outcrops the Eildons originated in upwellings of molten rocks which never penetrated the old layers of sandstones and conglamerites. Rather they cooled below the surface, where, after eons of erosion had removed the surrounding softer rock were left exposed as high points in the terrain, providing ideal sites for fortified camps and later peel towers and castles.

Other than on the coast there are few places where the old sandstone layers are exposed, there presence is best detected in the local housing material which until the relatively recent introduction of bricks was almost entirely of local origin. Travellers on the A1 may note the bright red sandstone

House in Lauder, whinstone with sandstone facings

of Ayton Castle. Further inland a lighter buff colour pre-
dominates, while in upland areas the hard unyielding whinstone
is sometimes dressed into square blocks. Here the easily worked
sandstone, known as 'freestone' for these properties, is used
in raising corners, window openings and door facings, the
remainder of the building formed from random rubble —
field — river stones or whatever was available. Often these
types of walls were and are disguised by 'harling' or some
modern method of this technique of coating undressed stone
with a mixture of cement/lime sand and fine gravel.

Surrounded by uplands the Borders represents something of
an enclave cut off from the heavy industries of the Tyne and
the Scottish Central Belt. Nor did it have the mineral resources
to exploit such industries, as only in a few places have men dug
below the ground in search of wealth, although coal has been
dug in a few places.

Agriculture has traditionally been the backbone of the
Borders' economy, which is not surprising, as within the area
are to be found some of the most fertile acres of agricultural

Uplands, Cocklawfoot shepherding in snow

land in Britain. Away from, and even on the fertile lowlands, farming is becoming less attractive, with sons and daughters now less keen to follow the family calling. Farms which come on the market today are more likely to be purchased by money from outwith the Borders, and even outwith the farming industry, bought for leisure use as much as food production. From 1988 to 1991 full-time male employment in agriculture throughout the entire Borders Region fell by 30 per cent. A prediction from a study carried out by the Scottish Agriculture College suggests that 2,000 further farming jobs will vanish over the next 25 years as a massive 740,000 acres of Border's farmland becomes surplus to requirements.

This is equally the case on uplands where sheep farming has long been a way of life, while in the early 1990s the market price of sheep has fallen in real and actual terms. Despite the image of wool from the black-faced sheep reared upon what is sometimes a bleak moorland going direct into the Border Mills in modern terms this does not occur. Native fleeces are only suitable for a minor part of the knitwear and weaving industry, much of the raw wool having to be imported for finer garments and cloths.

Around the four abbeys founded by King David the early agricultural improvement began with these religious houses being actively involved in the wool trade of the time.

Textiles now employ 18 per cent of the workforce. Again we are talking of the entire Borders Region although it was never of the same importance in the eastern March as further west. Electronics have become a rising star, helping to keep the unemployment rate well below the Scottish average.

Encouraging new industry and investment in the Borders is a role taken up by Scottish Borders Enterprise, whose area is the same as that of the Borders Regional Council. Borders Enterprise sees itself as having the following mission: 'To maintain the prosperity and to generate the economic growth of existing and additional enterprises in the Scottish Borders by encouraging the development of businesses and individual skills, whilst maintaining the total quality culture of life within the region'. Scottish Borders Enterprise will need to ensure that suitable premises are available for potential industrialists, which includes looking at the renovation of some of the old textile mills now standing idle or empty. Their job will be made easier by the strong regional identity and a continuing co-operation between educational establishments and in general the co-ordination between all bodies concerned with the wellbeing of the region. On the debit side the Borders has a long history of low wage rates, a restricted labour pool, which, along with the poor communication links and inadequate infrastructure SBE will strive to alleviate.

Tourism throughout the Region is rising in importance, bringing in some £50 million annually. The trend is changing with more activity-type holidays now available, bringing a different younger type of holidaymaker. Walking is superb in the Border Country. The hills may not be as challenging as in the Highlands but on the bonus side neither are they as crowded as the English Lakes. Off the main roads the touring cyclist can concentrate on routes with little motor traffic, or equipped with an all-terrain or mountain bike can explore the thread of drove roads and tracks crossing from valley to valley.

Walking is excellent in Borders, The Street one foot in Scotland one in England on Cheviot watershed

Where remains of major castles are rare in the Borders, taking Berwick, Bamburgh and Norham in Northumbria in contrast, the fortified house in various forms is found almost everywhere. In the years following Flodden the Scottish Borders were naked and vulnerable to attack, leading to an act being declared by the Scottish Parliament decreeing that every Scottish Borderer owning land to the value of £100 must embark upon the building of fortifications. These would consist of a 'barmkyn' or outer wall where cattle could be secured and a tower at least 60 feet square for the owner and his close staff.

Almost every drop of rain which falls in this area reaches the sea through the Tweed estuary at Berwick. The Eye Water is independent of Tweed, rising in the Lammermuirs before being thrust south by Coldingham Moors to flow by Reston and Ayton to enter the sea at Eyemouth. Tweed still flows much as it has done for the past two hundred years. Caulds — a local name for weir where the 'd' is often silent — may now be redundant where mill power is concerned, but remain they must if the present stream bed of the river is to be retained. Stream and pool the Tweed and its tributaries may bare her bones in summer drought or roar down in heavy flood, as happened in August 1948. Extensive damage

Tweed in 1948 Flood Coldstream Bridge (G. W. Gibson Coldstream)

was wrought upon road and rail bridges, the destruction of the latter bringing premature closure to several branch lines which never re-opened. Large numbers of farm stock were drowned. Fortunately there was no loss of human life, although there were some narrow escapes as was experienced by Bob Welsh then a gamekeeper at, and still living at Abbey St Bathans beside the Whiteadder. Described in Bob's own words:

Heavy rain had fallen throughout the night of 11th of August continuing into the next day, it was even too wet for a gamekeeper to be out so instead I had driven my employer to Duns on business. As we were returning we came into sight of Cockburn Law when we both remarked upon the amount of water streaming off the hill.

Back at the house the Whiteadder had risen, reaching to the lower of the 18 steps leading to the upstairs flat over some garages, where I lived with my wife Elizabeth and 16-month-old daughter Deborah. We had two guests at the weekend — my wife's niece Elizabeth Pow and a friend up on a fishing holiday, Mr Cowper from Darlington.

The house had just been wired for electricity and in fact it had only been switched on that day. I even remember that it was rabbit pie for tea that night, a particular favourite of Mr Cowper's. Somehow despite having seen the Whiteadder rise almost to the flat's steps in the past, for some reason I felt uneasy.

Suddenly there was a roar outside and looking out of the window I saw we were marooned, the raging flood water reaching almost to

13

Bob Welsh of Abbey St Bathans, Bob is standing beside the Whiteadder, 6ft mark on the gauge is some 3ft below the base level of Bob's house which stood nearby, the flat some 18 steps above that

the flat windows. Later it was confirmed that a log jam of debris and trees had given way upstream releasing the lake it had held back in a sudden rush.

Straight away I phoned Duns police station trying to stress the urgency of our situation. The call was only made in the nick of time, as with a crash the bathroom which stood on stilts behind the house broke free to float past the window carying the telephone line with it. By 6 p.m. the situation was getting desperate as the house was battered by debris, from hen houses to large trees, a large oak tree standing in a field upstream shed the debris to either side saving the house from instant destruction.

By 7 o'clock the water was still rising and cracks were appearing in the living room walls. There was nothing else for it but to seek a higher refuge which meant getting everyone out on the roof. What we did not know at the time was that the police were busy trying to get the Berwick coastguard team to The Abbey over flooded roads and destroyed bridges.

While we were on the roof there was another roar as the garage doors below were swept away along with the two cars and lorry, none of which were ever seen again. A group of people had gathered on dry land, including my mother and brother, but there was nothing anyone could do as no swimmer or even a boat could have withstood the flood. Someone had positioned their car so as the headlights shone on the roof, where, despite the situation, we remained calm.

The coastguard arrived at three in the morning and put a rocket line across the roof at the first attempt. The heavy line followed, then the rope and chair. In just over fifteen minutes we were all safely on firm land. We lost about everything we owned in the flood and received nothing from our insurers. The house was so badly damaged it had to be demolished, but it stood where the car park for the trout farm is now.

That is but one experience of 1948. Little wonder that when people of the eastern Borders talk about, 'The Flood' it does not refer to the biblical incident involving The Ark, but the local 1948 event which left the beach at Spittal deep in debris and stock carcasses.

Rising waters on the lower part of the Tweed can arrive on a summers day with never a cloud in the sky as a 'flash spate', the result of a 'thunner plump' fifty miles away in the hill areas. Wise anglers keep a wary eye on water levels when fishing from Tweed islands when rain is forecast around the uplands.

Drainage has changed the low lands beyond all recognition of how nature left them; grazing has eliminated the natural regeneration of forest in uplands. Of the old marshland only isolated pockets can be seen with one of the principal areas near Gordon at Gordon Moss Wildlife Reserve.

Remnants of natural woodland are equally difficult to find but fine examples can be seen in the stunted oak trees around Abbey St Bathans in the Whiteadder Valley. Yet, writing in the nineteenth century in *The Rivers of Scotland*, Sir Dick Lauder considered that remnants of the ancient forest of Caledeon could still be found in the upper reaches of the River Jed.

Few natural lochs are found here, at Yetholm, Hoselaw, and surprisingly above the cliffs north of St Abbs Head on the coast. The remaining areas of still water are artificial lochs in the shape of water supply reservoirs — a new feature this century. Many estates created artificial areas of stillwater on their estates, mainly as a decorative feature, some of which could also utilise the supply as a power source for machinery.

River valleys form a thread throughout the Borders reaching from the Tweed back into the uplands to start or end from bog or peat hag, a trickle — a burn — a stream to a river in its own right. Tweed itself has a more dignified source at Tweed's Well below Annanhead Hill rising from a recognisable spring. Cor Water, its first tributary, is the major stream, but Tweed it is from moorland to salt water.

In this landscape can be found a wide diversity of habitat supporting an appropriate selection of flora and fauna each occupying its own niche in Nature's system. Huge colonies of sea fowl are found along the steep coastal cliffs, on moorland where summertime larks sing the daylong the red grouse and curlew hold sway, ever alert for the stooping peregrine falcon. Occasionally ospreys are seen on passage, young unpaired birds sometimes spending the summer on the Tweed. The entire list of wild birds is much too extensive to pursue here.

Roe deer are the largest wild mammal, the fox the largest predator. Badgers are not uncommon; otters are present but seldom seen, while the feral mink has become one of the greatest threats to young waterfowl of all species. In intensive grain growing areas the brown hare population has dwindled, its decrease blamed on modern farming practices. The rabbit, however, has recently made a comeback, while in some parts of the Borders the population has reached infestation levels not seen since pre-myxomatosis days in the 1950s, and is again a threat to crops.

All Tweed's tributaries contain a head of brown trout, many having also runs of sea-trout and salmon. Minnows are plentiful in most streams but few have any appreciable stocks of coarse fish, other than grayling, in reality a member of the salmon family but considered by many trout anglers as a coarse fish.

Rivers within the Tweed system, even those in England, are governed by various Tweed Acts where the Tweed Commissioners are the responsible body for preserving salar the king of fishes. Salmon runs have changed within living memory with a decline in spring runs beginning in the 1960s accelerated by UDN which decimated these stocks. Summer fish and grilse declined in the 1980s with the main emphasise now on autumn fish.

Junction Pool Kelso, boatman is unhooking spring salmon for Florence
Miller

A number of special 'Tweed Acts' control all commercial and
sporting activities directed against salmon entering the Tweed
system. Among these is the total banning of the use of the gaff
for landing fish and special rules governing the methods used,
which vary according to the time of year.

Fishing for spring salmon which starts in winter at the
beginning of February, is restricted to artificial fly only for
the first two weeks when at one time the net fishing began on
the lower river. This form of fly fishing is far from a delicate
affair normally associated with the gentle art. Powerful rods and
fast sinking lines are employed to present the fly to the depths
of the pools where salmon lie in cold water conditions. Flies are
usually dressed on tubes, a hollow metal cylinder often bound
with lead wire for quicker sinking, the exotic plumes of the past
now replaced with dyed animal hair such as bucktail.

Even here the regulations differ between the prime mid-beats
of the Tweed and the public water of the upper reaches where
special rules have been adopted to eliminate foul hooking. As
the water temperature rises tackle becomes lighter, spinning

Tranquility, trout angling at Coldstream

is allowed until mid-September when the fly-only rule again comes into force when fishing for autumn fish through into the depths of winter at the season end on 31 November.

Salmon anglers renting a beat on the Tweed are usually accompanied by, not as is the case in the highlands, a gillie, but a boatman. The easy life of the Highland gillie lying at his ease on the bank encouraging his angler to wade even deeper, and cast even further if fish are to be caught, is not for the Tweed boatman. As is suggested by this term most of the fishing takes place afloat. With deceptively easy oar strokes the boatman keeps station over the places in the river where he knows salmon rest. Dropping down a few feet after every cast the boatman ensures that even an unskilled angler is covering every likely salmon holding spot or 'lie' in the pool.

Boatmen are known for their pawky sayings, like one who had returned to the fishing hut for his lunch leaving two anglers insistent upon continuing fishing. Enter the first angler dripping wet, 'what happened you?' enquired the boatman. 'I was lucky' replied the angler, 'I fell in. If X [the other angler] had not pulled me out I would not be here.' 'Aye' said the boatman, 'you're lucky to be here, awething that bugger ever hauled on the bank afore got a rap on the heid.'

Angling is followed with an almost religious fervour by many Borderers, not for the mighty salmon but in pursuit of the brown trout where perhaps for every line cast for salmon ten are directed against the trout. Costing on a prime beat at peak season a four-figure sum for a week, salmon angling on the Tweed is beyond the pocket of most local anglers.

Fortunately this does not apply to trout fishing with local clubs and associations controlling trout angling rights on many miles of water. These are listed in the *Angling Guide to the Scottish Borders* and *Scotland for Fishing*. Both publications are available from tourist information offices throughout the Borders. Brown trout fishing, especially on the Tweed, can prove extremely difficult at times; today if success is to be ensured it is to the dry or floating fly that the angler must turn. This is a complete reversal of the situation over the past four decades when it was possible to take a respectable basket of trout from the Tweed with wet or sunk fly representing an aquatic insect prior to its hatching upon the surface. Trout seem to find this nymphal stage of water-borne insects less attractive these days; now it is only when hatching flies dot the surface that there is any sign of feeding activity.

Perhaps the Tweed is becoming much more fertile, producing more food on the bottom than was previously the case. Post-mortems upon trout caught on a tiny dry fly on a summer's evening usually reveal that previously the fish had been gorging upon a mixture of bottom dwelling freshwater snails, caddis larvae and freshwater shrimps.

Many notable anglers have fished and written on trout angling in the Borders, Stewart, W. H. Lawrie and Stoddart being the best known. Also of course Canon Greenwell from Durham who asked Sprouston fly dresser James Wright to tie him a fly in the imitation of the dark olive. Wright produced a simple fly of yellow waxed silk body ribbed with gold wire, furnace hackle and blackbird wing the 'Greenwells Glory' the most famous trout fly of all time. Greenwell's name is immortal but outside trout angling circles few know of the Glory's creator who lies buried in Sprouston churchyard.

Like trout fishing, golf around the Border courses is not the prerogative of the wealthy or professional class; club courses are within the financial reach of anyone who can afford a set of clubs. Nor is there any snobbery attached to the game here, while the courses themselves, from the secluded Hirsel at Coldstream (currently undergoing expansion into an 18-hole course), Eyemouth's cliff top setting to the airy Hardens at Duns, offer superb facilities, especially when the moderate cost is considered. All club courses in the Borders are also open to visitors.

Of the old burghs and towns featured in this book, Jedburgh, Melrose, Earlston and Kelso are all established rugby strong-holds. Duns is a relative newcomer to the oval ball game, as is Berwick on Tweed. Elsewhere, at Coldstream and Eyemouth, soccer is the name of the game on a winter Saturday. Soccer even in the rugby heartland has its enthusiasts and teams.

Although Scotland and England have been united in crowns for almost four and in parliaments for three centuries the accent between the two countries remains distinctive. For example at Coldstream a mere stones skip over the Tweed, the Border accent and bilingual ability on the Scottish side, and the

Northumbrian burr at Cornhill a mile distant are immediately obvious. Throughout Berwickshire the vowel sounds are broad, yet the turn of phrase and idiom can be entirely different in the coastal towns and villages.

*The Guid Scots Tongue* by David Muirison gives the dialect for this eastern part of The Borders as East Mid Scots; south-west into Teviotdale by the Yarrow valley and extending to the Solway it changes to Southern Scots.

What is shared by the people on either side of the Border is the art of the understatement. Praise from a Borderer should be guarded with suspicions, what would elsewhere be hailed as grand, be it a social occasion, a sporting event or the capture of a trout of undreamt of dimensions and weight is described by the Borderer as, 'no bad'. Mistaken for dourness by the unfamiliar, but as so much superlative can happen here, the Borderer saves the, 'superbs and fantastics' for some really worthy future event.

Local festivals are a unique feature in the Borders; in the area dealt with in this book only Lauder has a traditional Riding of the Marches, — a Common Riding. The mounted festival extends to most other towns which once enjoyed burgh status. Although some of these events are of fairly recent origin, such is the history of the Borders that most manage to incorporate a visit to some site of historic importance as in Coldstream's Flodden Cavalcade and Jedburgh's Redeswire Ride.

Horseback festivals follow the Common Riding pattern of electing a young man to carry the burgh flag for the week's celebrations. In Duns The Riever also has a Riever's Lass — in Kelso the Kelsae Laddie or a name appropriate to the town such as The Coldstreamer or Melrosian.

It takes some commitment to engage upon this official festival role of leader, as in many cases it requires a three-year stint as right-hand man, leader, then left-hand man. Nor is it an inexpensive matter as it is expected that the three principles support and attend rideouts at other mounted festivals of which there are eleven throughout the Borders Region.

Appropriately the village of Swinton alongside where map makers emblazon Merse upon their sheets, the village festival is centred upon the coronation of the Queen of the Merse. Just about every village manages a festival week or at least a Gala day aimed mainly at the youth and the election of a young girl as queen.

Lying within a circle of hills, roads since the earliest times have perforce been required to follow the lines of least resistance. River valleys reaching up to low points in the skyline have been obvious routes since time immemorial; such roads by their nature seeking the easiest of gradients twist and turn in their search.

Principal lines of communication from north to south transverse The Borders; the main east coast railway, now electrified, hugs the coastal strip in Berwickshire. This it shares with the A1, a road link which in the opinion of many drivers is sadly in need of updating to at least dual carriageway status.

From the Tyne valley the A68 and A696 (T) rise up through Redesdale to become the A68 (T), once over the Carter Bar by way of Jedburgh and St Boswells, crossing the Tweed at Leaderfoot Bridge. Following the ancient line through Lauderdale the A68 (T) climbs over the Lammermuirs at Soutra Hill, notorious in snow, before dropping into the Lothians.

Skirting the eastern edge of the Cheviots by Wooler and Coldstream the A697 combines with the A68 (T) at Carfraemill while the A7 (T) follows Border Esk and Teviot from Longtown in Cumbria to Hawick — Galashiels then onwards by Gala Water to Edinburgh. East to west roads are tedious throughout the Borders. Despite their A category they are in fact little more than country roads, even although sections have been and are in the process of being improved.

Nevertheless the Borders is suitable country for the motorist; heavy traffic densities are rare away from the towns and arterial roads. Frustrations of tail backs and hours in traffic jams do not in normal circumstances occur on the Border roads. Armed with a good road map or better still the appropriate Ordnance Survey Landranger, it is possible to explore the B class and unclassified roads throughout the Region.

Backroads and byeroads thread through the farming heartland serving villages and farms, through the valleys of Tweed's tributaries to climb over the Lammermuirs into East Lothian. Others skirt the verge of the Cheviot Hills making shortcuts in miles if not time for drivers who seek the quietness away from the more popular tourist routes. Talking of which the Leisure

Anne Browne of Radio Tweed interviewing Lauder Cornet

Map for Borders England and Scotland covers all major roads and lists in addition sites of special interest to the visitor.

Once the thread of railways served the Borders, branch lines penetrated up river valleys to towns and villages. The Beeching cuts in the sixties severed all these, including the Waverley Line from Galashiels to Edinburgh. Today there are no railway stations within the Region; travellers by train must proceed from the mainline station at Berwick on Tweed which remains well served by Intercity routes.

Commercial radio and television coverage in the area is served by Carlisle-based Borders Television and Radio Borders from Tweedbank near Melrose. Radio Borders only opened in the spring of 1990 but in its first year of operation the station received the distinction of being nominated the most listened to local station, in terms of population of its area, in a survey conducted by Official Audience Research.

Further honours came in 1991 when in the face of competition from 140 local stations throughout Britain Radio Borders received the, 'Sony Radio Award' as the Best Local

Station of the Year. Radio Borders from its Tweedbank base near Melrose broadcasts some 105 hours of its own news, local magazine and music programmes but through the, 'Max A. M. station is on the air 24 hours a day.

From a base in Selkirk the BBC's Border outpost, BBC Tweed, provides an hour of daily programmes directed to the Borders, but contributes also to network broadcasting such as the magazine programme the Tweed Gathering, the Border's answer to Jimmy Macgregor.

Education in the eastern March lies in the hands of the Borders Region through a primary and high school network, with the Borders College for those beyond school-leaving age. At Duns and St Boswells the branches of the Borders College offer courses suitable for students seeking employment in the area. Course of study aimed at Scotvec National Certificates are available at both centres, including agriculture, agricultural engineering, horticulture, horse management and gamekeeping. Scotvec courses in office administration and technology are also on hand, while Borders Flexitec provides computer training from word processing and accounting to basic programming.

Always resilient, today this part of the Borders looks to the future. Farming may be in decline, the coastal fishing industry under threat, but as they have done in the past the people will adapt to new opportunities. Down through the centuries such has been the way of the Borderer.

# CHAPTER 2

## *Coastal*

Coastal Berwickshire, the Borders seaward boundary, joins that of East Lothian, where the Dunglass Burn enters the sea at Bilsdean Creek. Cut by steep ravines, squeezed seawards by the Lammermuirs, at present the narrow coastal strip has three different road bridges of varying vintage carrying the Edinburgh-London road across Dunglass Burn. A fourth bridge is under construction on the Cockburnspath bypass, while somehow the railway has also managed to appropriate enough room for its progress.

Dunglass Collegiate Church is well signposted from the A1, reached by passing under the railway bridge on a section of what was once the main road. Despite being used as a barn in the eighteenth century the building is surprisingly intact due in part to its construction form of barrel vaulting and stone slabbed roof, meaning that there was little to decay other than the weathering of the stone by natural forces.

Founded in the 1440s as a chapel dedicated to St Mary by Sir Alexander Home of Dunglass, the church was not a place of public worship, but devoted entirely to the saying of mass for the souls of the kings of Scotland, the Bishop of St Andrews and the family of the founder who had granted lands to maintain the chapel and clergy. The burial place of the Home family lies in the north transept, the Halls in the south transept.

Sir James Hall (1761–1832) the 4th baronet and owner of Dunglass was an agricultural improver, and an associate of the geologists Hutton and Playfair. The naked exposure of the Silurian and Old Devonian red sandstone on the nearby coast was no doubt an inspiration to their further studies.

Cockburnspath, locally Copath, anciently Coldbrandspaith, is the eastern end of the Southern Upland Way which has threaded its way from Portpatrick, near Stranraer, into and through the Borders. James IV gave the lands of Cockburns-path to his bride Margaret Tudor in 1503, erecting the market

25

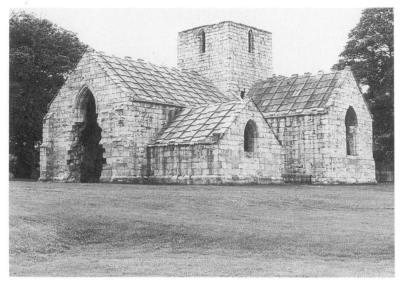

Dunglass Collagiate Church

cross, now the official terminus of the Way, to commemorate
the event. Created a free burgh in 1612 the inhabitants of
that time had the right to hold a weekly market, an annual
Lammas Fair, hold courts and elect their own burgesses and
bailiffs.

Cove harbour is the seaport for Cockburnspath, if such a
term can be applied to the tiny basin which maintains one of
the smallest fleets of full-time fishing boats in Scotland. Cove
is a secretive place, a half mile of rough track from the village
above. The two inhabited houses are reached through a tunnel
hewn through the sandstone cliffs.

Part of the harbour is cut from the living rock which also
forms the basin, making it a most unsuitable place for small
boats to lie, due the the pounding taken when they ground
with the ebbing tide, or begin to float with the flood. Four
fishermen manning the two boats still berthed here sail daily
when weather permits in search of crabs and lobsters. In the
past Cove has seen busier times where the fishing industry is
concerned. At the time of what is sometimes called the East

Cove Harbour, popular as a summer sun spot

Coast Disaster on 13 October 1881, eleven fishermen and four boats were lost from this tiny haven.

Fishing at Cove goes back as far as at least the 1600s and perhaps beyond, increased effort in earlier years being curtailed by the lack of a proper harbour. During the 1750s Sir John Hall, the laird of nearby Dunglass, engaged a contractor to construct a breakwater to provide some protection for moored vessels. These works were never fully completed, being destroyed by the fury of a north-east gale.

What was achieved at the time was the cutting of the now familiar tunnel through the rock. Originally there were storage chambers also in here, but these have been bricked up in recent years. A road was also constructed at this time, basically the same as is used today. Further work on encouraging the fishing industry at Cove proceeded over the years, heavy seas destroying these, until in 1831 the present basin with its seawalls and breakwaters was completed. In these times sea transport was of some importance in general trade, with ships of up to sixty tons berthing at Cove when weather conditions allowed.

Outward the main cargo would be agriculture produce — grain and wool — inwards coal, lime and perhaps building materials not available locally. Coal had been mined at Dunglass and Cove but the enterprise was short lived and the quality poor being used only for burning lime and by the poor. When the railway reached the east coast with a station at nearby Cockburnspath, the coasting trade died and Cove reverted to being purely a fishing harbour.

What the rocky coast is suitable for is the catching of shellfish by the traditional method of a baited creel or pot. Tight in along the low water mark, among drying rock and reef, is the favourite haunt of the most prized of all shellfish, the lobster. There is little evidence that lobsters migrate any great distance, possibly being present inshore the year round. It is for only a few months of the year (in Berwickshire from August to November) that large numbers of lobster are willing to enter baited traps.

Like all crustacea the lobster is encased in a hard unyielding shell which has within no provision for growth; to increase its size the existing shell must be discarded leaving below a vulnerable soft-as-butter body. Aware of the conditions in the sea bed jungle when those unable to defend themselves are liable to become a ready meal, the lobster retreats into a cranny among rocks or boulders while the new shell hardens and becomes once more a suit of armour. Hungry after this enforced period of hibernation the water-borne scent of a ripe cod's head or salted mackerel drifting downtide from a baited creel is now irresistible. Like their colleagues all along the Berwickshire Coast creel fishermen at Cove are beset by a number of problems threatening their livelihood. What is the least expected by the layman is the mass slaughter of lobsters by octopus. Yes, octopus, those jet-propelled ink-squirting things with eight arms or legs, depending upon how you define these multiple appendages.

Thankfully their dimensions are nowhere like those which film makers depict, reaching over the boat's rail to haul an unsuspecting mariner to a watery grave. Rather they are about the size of a deflated football, but since 1988 they have killed thousands of lobsters within fishermen's creels. Slaughter of lobsters can occur without the octopus entering the creel;

the eight arms versus two claws is no contest, the lobster being clutched against the mesh for the injection of lethal venom before consumption.

Further problems in the creel fishery are found in the decline of crab catches which for part of the year formed a major part of the income for inshore fishermen. Compound this with a stagnation in shellfish prices partially brought on by the arrival of cheap Canadian lobsters on European markets traditionally supplied from Scotland, and it is not difficult to see why there is little cause for optimism in this sector of the fishing industry at the moment.

Cove harbour came into public ownership when Dunglass Estates gifted the area to the old Berwickshire Council. From there upon the regionalisation of local government Cove passed to the Borders Regional Council. During the late 1980s controversy arose around Cove because of the Regional Council's closure of the access road to vehicle traffic.

This was done on grounds of public safety due to the continual erosion of the cliffs below the road, the closure effectively blocking off the fishermen from their boats with the need to transport fuel and bait down to and their catch up from the harbour. Since then the road has been re-opened for fishermen to use, and Cove Harbour has been purchased by an Edinburgh architect. This follows something of a false start when an earlier prospective purchaser had his plans for developing a marina complex at Cove turned down by the Regional Planning Department.

From the verge of the Lothians the coastline rises towards Coldingham Moors, outliers of the Lammermuirs sliced from the main upland body by the Pease Burn and Eye Valley. Prior to it being bridged Heriot Water and Pease Dene (as the deep valley of this latter burn is called) was long a major obstacle on the north–south route. Cromwell considered it a place, 'where ten men to hinder are better than forty to make their way'. The remains of Cockburnspath or Dunglass Tower stand beside the Heriot Water, assumed to be Scott's Ravenswood in *The Bride of Lammermoor*.

As we have seen there is evidence that three or perhaps four relatively modern roads are to be found passing near Cockburnspath. This was always a major route north for invading armies; beyond were the major castles of Dunbar, Tantallon and Direlton, with Edinburgh and the Lothians beyond. When Cospatrick obtained Dunbar and Cockburnspath Castles he was said, 'to have held the keys of Scotland at his girdle'.

Pease Dene was formed during the last Ice Age when meltwater flowing below the sheet ice gouged a gully through soft sandstone and shales. The name Pease is said to derive from paths cut diagonally up the steep sides of the ravine. The situation was not always fully exploited by the Scots, as Hertford returned through the Pease with little hindrance following his 1544 raid, despite a Scottish force which included Home and Buccleuch pricking and harrying his force during thick fog.

With financial aid from the Nature Conservancy Council, The World Wide Fund for Nature and the Countryside Commission for Scotland the Scottish Wild Life Trust were able in 1988 to purchase Pease Dene and establish the site as a Wildlife Reserve. In the cool moist habitat below the mature trees myriads of wild flowers flourish amid a bed of ferns, lichen and mosses. Overhead the decaying elms provide an ample opportunity for the greater spotted woodpecker to sound out its territorial claims or drill a spring nesting hole.

Conservation plans for the Dene, which is a regular feature of ranger led walks, include the removal of some of the introduced conifers, allowing native trees and shrubs to flourish where eventually the 75-acre site will be one of the largest deciduous woods in Berwickshire.

Pease Bay is one of only three easily accessible sandy beaches along Berwickshire's east coast, a sprawling caravan site occupying the flat land and hillside inland from the beach. While it could be described as something of a blot, it is secluded and no doubt provides many families with a fairly peaceful holiday.

South from Pease the landscape takes on an appearance typical of the Merse coastline, high cliffs plunging either to the sea or to rocky beaches. From Pease Bay to St Abbs Head can be found one of the best cliff-top walks in Britain. Wild and remote, however, it should only be undertaken by experienced walkers.

A mile or so from Pease Bay the gable and walls of a

ruined church can be seen — Auldcambus or St Helen's on the lea.

> St Abbs, St Helen and St Bey
> They all built kirks to be nearest the sea
> St Abb's upon the Nabbs, St Helen's on the lea
> St Ann's upon Dunbar sands,
> Stands nearest to the sea.

St Helen's is mainly a Norman structure but at the beginning of the nineteenth century it is said that a small Saxon arch was to be found at the entrance to the chancel. Auldcambus church is first mentioned in 1097 but it is possible that an even earlier building occupied the site. Local legend has it that a leper hospital was near St Helens, the lone ruins of the church marking the site of a now vanished village of Auldcambus.

Siccar Point lies close to hand, where in the late eighteenth century Berwickshire man James Hutton fitted together another piece of the jigsaw to build the complete picture for his book, *History of the Earth.*

Hutton believed that the rocks of the earth's surface were in a constant state of being either made or destroyed by natural forces. Published in 1785 this book flew in the face of all previous theories on geological science. Sea erosion exposing the very bones of the earth at Siccar, revealed to Hutton the vertical folded slabs of Silurian rocks capped by horizontal red sandstone indicating that in the past separated by millions of years great forces had been brought to bear.

Not all fishing activity in this part of the world was carried out from Cove, as below the impressive outcrop of Redheugh fishermen once sailed from this somewhat hazardous shore. Although removed in the 1700s the trade was continuing in 1802 with four boats working. In more recent times the shore and boathouse have been used as a salmon fishing station working 'bag nets', but the fishery was later pursued from Cove on the replacement of the pulling boats by motorised vessels.

Smuggling appears to have been a sideline here, or was it the main business! A row of coastguard houses stands high on the shore keeping watch on this rugged and seldom visited coast. Lady Helen Hall of Dunglass records in her journal, 'the trade at Redheugh has never been fishing, but smuggling, which has been put a stop to'.

From Dowlaw farm, indicated on the Berwickshire coastal route from Burnmouth to Tower Bridge at Cockburnspath, a track past the cottages, then a quite easily followed path, leads to Fast Castle Head. Perched on the headland are the few remnants of what must have been a grim forbidding outpost — Fast Castle. Around these remains legends abound, treachery, buried treasure and the romance of Scott who based Wolf's Craig in *The Bride of Lammermoor* upon Fast Castle.

Modern interest in Fast Castle began in the late 1960s when an Edinburgh man, Fred Douglas, instigated a search for the gold bullion said to be hidden there. Not that he was the first, as the search extends back to at least 1596, when John Napier, the inventor of logarithms, entered a contract with Fast Castle's owner, Robert Logan, to discover the hidden treasure.

Despite searching by land and sea no trace of treasure has been found at Fast Castle. More importantly, the story inspired the Edinburgh Archaeological Field Society to conduct a more scientific dig, unearthing in the process a number of interesting relics and new information on the site. What they failed to find was any passage connecting the Castle to the large cave below, the stairway within the castle shell coming to an abrupt end.

A detailed report of the Society's 16-year-long 'dig' was published in 1988, recording their work, artifacts recovered and the history of Fast Castle and the surrounding area. Up until 1871 it appears as if some fabric of the building remained when a lightning strike completed the earlier work of siege and weather. Surrounded on three sides by the sea, walled by steep cliffs, reached from the landward side across a narrow gap by a ramp, there is little wonder that Fast Castle Head was a natural choice for a defensive building.

Seventy feet above sea level bounded by steep cliffs the 260ft × 88ft wide Fast Castle Head was safe from seaborne attack and should, prior to cannon, have required siege to starve the occupants into surrender. Yet Fast Castle changed hands many times during the years of cross-Border warfare, sometimes in Scottish at others in English hands.

Siege and attack by supporters of the Scots or English featured over the centuries at Fast Castle. Possibly supplies

Fast Castle

could be replenished by sea and there was said by Hector Boece in *Bounds of Albion* to be a stone held here with wondrous properties: 'In this crag was sum time ane stane, full of ene and holis, like ane water spounge, holkit in the middis, of sik nature, that all salt watter that is waschin thairwith becumis incontinent fresche and delicius to the mouth'.

Capture of the castle between warring factions was not always by full scale siege. Held in 1548 by the English, a Scottish force under one John Robertson disguised themselves as the local husbandmen who were being forced to victual and carry peats for fuel into the castle. With weapons concealed below clothing the 'innocent' peasants attacked and held the gates, defying the defenders until the main band arrived to wrest control.

Both the good and evil found shelter below its roof after the trek across Coldingham Moor heading north. Margaret Tudor spent a night at Fast Castle, when, in 1503, on her way north to wed James IV, princess Margaret was said to be in 'grete chere' while being entertained at 'Barwyk', what her mood was after a night spent at Fast Castle is not recorded.

A final tragic tale from this lonely spot was the execution of a Eyemouth notary, George Sprott, who had been drawn into the peripheral of the Gowrie conspiracy to either murder James VI, or take him captive to Fast Castle. Robert Logan of Fast Castle, laird also of Restalrig and proprietor of Gunsgreen House in Eyemouth was however a willing partner in the kidnap plot.

Fast Castle seems to have been a meeting place for the

conspirators, whom the unfortunate Sprott was visiting when he overheard a conversation or a letter being read aloud by Logan, concerning the Gowrie plot. Letters between Logan and Gowrie were obtained by Sprott from one Bour the messenger between the plotters, whereafter Logan bribed Sprott with the sum of £12 to remain silent over the affair. After the deaths of Logan and Bour, both in 1606, Sprott two years later let drop in public some knowledge of the Gowrie plot and was arrested and dragged to Edinburgh. Confession of involvement by Sprott was obtained under torture, with the death sentence pronounced and carried out by hanging in public on 12 August 1608.

As early as 1905 the *Scottish Mountaineering Club Journal*, listed around 112 cliffs and stacks between Fast Castle and St Abbs Head, some given as between 400 and 500ft in height. Beaches below comprise rocks and boulders with only a few places where the non-mountaineer can descend safely to sea level.

Near Lumsden Farm the line of an old track zig-zags up the coast with below a primitive harbour where boats could be beached to unload cargoes such as coal and lime. Old beach stations for salmon were once worked around here, but as elsewhere this trade has now been abandoned.

A half-mile behind the cliff top mid-way between Fast Castle and St Abbs Head is the only naturally occurring Loch within the old Berwickshire county. Some 20 acres in extent, Coldingham Loch is entirely spring fed through sandstones and some limestones, making it, despite the proximity of moorland, a very fertile water supporting an abundance of aquatic life.

It is thought that fish stocks in the shape of perch were first introduced to Coldingham Loch by the monks of Coldingham Priory, ensuring a ready supply of fish essential for Friday meals. Today the perch introduced by the monks and able to breed in still water remain, along with the more recent stockings of brown and rainbow trout.

The concept of stocked waters for anglers is a popular one today, but it is probable that Coldingham can claim to be one of the first places in Scotland to introduce trout on a put-and-take basis purely for sporting purposes. Originally the fish were from the Loch Leven strain of brown trout, which, like rainbows, cannot breed in non-running waters. Coldingham

Loch is run as a day ticket water for anglers who travel from all around the Borders, Northumbria and Scotland's Central Belt to attempt the deception of Coldingham's trout.

Almost separated from its hinterland by the obvious fault of Mire Loch, the massif of St Abbs Head is a recent infiltrator of volcanic rock set among older sedimentaries. The headland bears the name of St Ebbe, the daughter of a Northumbrian king, Ethelfrith, her maternal uncle possibly Edwin, founder of Edinburgh. Ebbe or Ebba was said to have been fleeing by boat from the unwelcome courtship of one Penda, pagan king of Mercia, to be shipwrecked on the Berwickshire coast.

Of course, at the end of the seventh century it was not the Berwickshire but the Northumbrian coast, that kingdom in those days consisting of Bernicia — Forth to Tees, and Deira — Tees to Humber. Which is a bit beside the point in the story that she established the nunnery on the bleak headland to give thanks for her salvation. A more inhospitable place to survive a shipwreck than below the cliffs of St Abbs Head would be difficult to find.

There is a more creditable version in that the scene of the shipwreck was on Coldingham Sands and that Ebba established the religious house on the site of the present priory, the kirk on the headland being more a place for retreat and meditation. For the unromantic there is another account in that Ebbe founded the Church of Ebchester in County Durham sometime before 660 AD. This was destroyed by the Danes, and its royal foundress removed to Coldingham where she was made Abbess. St Ebbe died in 679 AD. Some two hundred years later, in 870 AD the convent was despoiled by Danish invaders, an event which gave birth to another legend of St Ebbe.

Hoping to discourage Viking lust the nuns were reputed to have mutilated their faces in the hope of being spared from what was to them a fate worse than death. Rough sculpted stones found in the churchyard at Coldingham Priory are said to represent the disfigurement of St Ebbe, which if this was the case must have been another Abbess to bear the name of the venerated seventh-century patron.

In contrast, John Renton in the *Statistical Account* relates the following story of the disfigurement: 'And by way of contrast to that very singular mode of preserving their chastity, it is said that the Pope, in some of his charters to the Convent, indulged the Monks with the use of some females for certain periods . . .'.

Before St Ebba arrived, giving her name to what was previously Coldburgh Head, early man had settled in a string of forts and camps all along the coastline. On St Abbs Head itself, human activity has waxed and waned over the years. Services, mainly maritime, have arrived and departed from the headland. These included coastguard and a semaphore station. This latter 'spoke' to ships entering the Forth through a semaphore tower. Messages concerning cargoes and e. t. a. were then relayed overland by telegraph.

Today only the keepers of St Abbs light, built in 1860, and one of the few remaining manned lighthouses on the east coast, keep their light burning on what was, before the introduction of modern navigation equipment, a vital guide into the Firth of Forth. Usually lighthouse keepers face an upwards climb when engaged in their duties. Such is the elevation of St Abbs light that the tower is actually some distance below the light keepers' houses, reached by a walled stairway.

Electrical power now rotates St Abbs light, emitting a flash every ten seconds, which, according to *Reed's Nautical Almanac*, 'has an elevation of 29 metres and in clear conditions is visible for 21 miles'. Before electricity the original driving power for most lighthouses was a mechanism similar to that found in long-case clocks, i.e., a weight first wound up by hand, then subject to the force of gravity descended under control, through a series of gears and pulleys finally to rotate the light mechanism at the desired speed.

Perched upon such an elevated site St Abbs light is a low structure, with no convenient tower for the mechanism; instead a well was dug underneath to provide the necessary drop for the weight. Part of the lighthouse keepers' duties at St Abbs is to record the weather conditions every hour for the 'Met'. Weather watchers may know that winds of over a hundred miles an hour are recorded here, especially when they sweep down the Firth of Forth to vent their fury upon the headland of St Ebbe.

With steep cliffs making them safe from ground predators St Abbs Head is an important nesting site for seabirds. Since 1980 the 192 acres on the headland have been under National Trust for Scotland ownership, known as the 'St Abbs Head

National Nature Reserve', managed in conjunction with the Scottish Wild Life Trust. Members of the auk family, guillemots and razorbills find the situation ideal for their special needs where chicks free fall from the nest into the sea. They do have to compete with a squabbling selection of other species. The courtship and nesting season is far from a quiet occasion as alongside the auks a selection of fulmars, kittiwakes and herring gulls make their feelings known in a concert of raucous crys.

Sea fowl are the most obvious in the Reserve, due no doubt in part to the above raucous cries, yet around thirty hedgerow and wetland species can be found elsewhere on the 192 acres, especially around the artificial Mire Loch. Natural flora form another important feature along the cliff tops, where artificial fertilisers and chemical sprays have not altered the composition of the soil.

The rare butterfly, the Northern Brown Argus, in whose life cycle the rock rose is so important, has itself received protection in a fenced off area, allowing it to thrive away from where the hardy black faced sheep still graze within the reserve. Following two dry summers in 1989 and 1990 the herbage on the reserve became seriously affected by drought conditions. This has led in 1991 to a suspension of grazing, resulting in an exceptional blooming of thrift carpeting the headland in a sea of pink.

Access to St Abbs Head Reserve is usually from the car park at Northfield Farm, and is well signposted on the B 6438 between Coldingham and St Abbs. A visitor centre can be found in the red tiled building just outside the car park which incorporates the 'Head Start' coffee shop. Regular ranger-led walks to 'seabird city' take place during the summer months and details are available from tourist offices throughout the Borders.

From Northfield the paths around the reserve are well signposted and obvious on the ground, offering no difficulty to any visitor who is reasonably fit and wears footwear appropriate for steep grass slopes. A vehicle road leads right up to the lighthouse where there is limited parking space, allowing access for disabled visitors here and at the Pettico Wick slipway in the Mire Loch fault.

Pettico Wick slipway was built in the days when, like other lights, that at St Abbs Head was replenished by sea through

St Abbs, George Wilson of Ailsa Jane landing damaged lobster creels

small boats from the steamship lying offshore. Pettico Wick was once a salmon station, long since closed, and its buildings razed, but the slipway remains in use by the many diving parties who visit this part of the reserve.

The waters around St Abbs Head are included in the Eyemouth and St Abbs Voluntary Marine Reserve extending from Pettico Wick to Eyemouth, where a special code of practice is aimed at protecting marine life. Again ranger led, 'rock pool rambles' are a summer feature where the life of the shoreline is explained.

Below the headland can be found the fishing village of St Abbs, on a site previously known as Coldingham Shore and still refered to simply as 'The Shore'. Of fairly modern origin, the harbour was built in 1833 on land granted by a brewing family; the trust deeds still prohibit the establishment of licensed premises for the consumption of alcohol.

Several of the larger boats owned by St Abbs fishermen are based at Eyemouth, just over a mile to the south, on a permanent basis. For the remainder their main target is

Mauritania undergoing sea trials below St Abbs Head
(John Wood Collection)

shellfish, inshore, as is the case all along the Berwickshire coast. This involves the use of the creel, known here as the crave or crib, aimed at crabs and lobsters.

Offshore into deeper water trawling for prawns (i.e., Norway lobsters or nephrops) is the principal occupation. Nephrops are familiar to most people as scampi which is the destiny of the smaller specimens; larger examples are usually exported whole to the Continent where there appears to be an insatiable demand for this delicacy.

Scuba diving is a popular pursuit from St Abbs harbour where the clear waters offer ideal conditions for this sport. With modern equipment, especially dry suits, diving is no longer merely a summer pastime, but on weekends throughout the year when conditions are favourable divers are likely to be found somewhere beneath the sea around St Abbs.

While it is without question that divers make a significant contribution to the tourist economy of St Abbs there is an opinion among some locals that their village is taken over by these visitors at peak periods.

Another of Berwickshire's few sandy beaches is found at Coldingham Sands, not surprisingly a popular spot during the summer months for those in search of sea, sand and most years a fair share of sun. Fine summer Sundays see the crowds of holidaymakers from Coldingham's two caravan sites swollen by day trippers from throughout the Borders to a state where even the large carpark above the Sands finds it difficult to cope.

Coldingham (invariably this is pronounced as Cowdenham locally), has already been mentioned earlier as being the original fisher town before St Abbs was established, and also having possible connections with St Ebbe. Today the choir, the only surviving part of the old Priory, forms the present-day parish church, probably dating from the early part of the eleventh century and replacing the building where St Ebbe was possibly Abbess.

Even after the Scottish Border was established at the Tweed, ecclesiastically Coldingham remained attached to Durham. It was not until five hundred years later that Coldinghamshire ceased to be an appendage of the See of Durham to which it had been attached by Edgar, King of Scots, in AD 1098. The term Coldinghamshire is first mentioned by the venerable Bede, and later accounts claim that Coldinghamshire was equal to an eighth part of the County of Berwick.

This usage of 'shire' in Coldinghamshire does not signify county but is a now undefinable division of church territory, in this instance perhaps meaning 'the parishes attached to Coldingham Priory'. Certainly these appear to have included Lamberton, Mordington, Foulden, Hutton and Paxton, Horndean, Ladykirk, Simprim, Swinton, and Whitsome — perhaps including Bonkyl Edrom and Chirnside.

The families of Home and Douglas featured prominently in the early days of Coldingham Priory, not always in agreement with each other it must be said. However, when James III decided to suppress Coldingham Priory to obtain funds for a Chapel-Royal at Stirling, the Homes, Hepburns, Argyle, Lennox and the Earl of Angus united against the royal decree, eventually defeating it.

Royalist forces held out for two days in 1648 against an attack by General Oliver Cromwell, who seemed to have a way with gunpowder where Priories and Abbeys were concerned,

Coldingham Village at turn of century
(John Wood Collection)

generally completing the ruin by blowing it up and leaving only
the tower intact. Later in 1662 part of the Choir was rebuilt to
form the present parish church.

Leaving Coldingham village on the road to St Abbs, at Fishers
Brae Garage is found one of most unique pictorial documents
of Scottish rural life in the late nineteenth and early twentieth
century. This, 'The John Wood Collection' is all the more
remarkable in the story of its survival.

Back in 1983, Roy Thomson then aged ten, son of the Fishers
Brae Garage owner, Robert Thomson, embarked upon a school
project portraying early twentieth-century life in the village of
Coldingham. Roy's research, with his father's assistance, led
to the door of Jimmy Brown, a retired market gardener who
had already given Robert some old postcards which as a keen
amateur photographer he had copied for his son's project.

Jimmy searched drawers and chests for more old postcards
but alas there were none, but, 'what about these?' These turned
out to be a box of old glass negatives, stored in a garden shed,

their purpose being to replace broken panes in greenhouses and cold frames.

Despite being covered with fifty years of dust and grime, one of the first plates removed from the box was of Coldingham village. It dawned on Robert Thomson that here was something unique and virtually priceless historically. Originally from Glasgow, John Wood had married a widow, Margaret Kerr, who kept a shop in the village, where Wood became established as a professional photographer.

Using a half-plate camera, Wood earned a living taking formal portraits of the inhabitants posed in their Sunday best, which would be the bread and butter of any rural photographer of the time. More importantly, perhaps for his own interest, he also recorded the everyday life of the village and surrounding district. The ploughmen, masons building a new hall, threshing days, even the S. S. *Mauretania* undergoing sea trials below St Abbs Head — to name but a few. With perfect focus, composition and slow speed the half plates still produce huge enlargements without grain. There is no disputing the fact that John Wood had talent when it came to photography.

The Thomson family, Robert, his wife Mary and and Roy have recovered six hundred usable plates from that dusty box, countless hours going into their cleaning and restoration to a condition suitable for printing to virtually any size using a seven foot high half plate enlarger.

What gives the Thomson family nightmares is the story told by a villager, Forsyth Lindores, of how as a young man John Wood's daughter asked him if he could make use of some old glass. Two lorry loads of glass negatives were removed for glazing or to be broken up among concrete for outhouse floors.

Each spring a new collection of prints is displayed in the gallery housing The John Wood Collection, maintained by means of donations, although entry is free. From the prints it can be seen that the centre of Coldingham has changed little since John Wood photographed the scene almost a hundred years ago. Standing beside the Market Cross opposite the Anchor Inn, French's horse-drawn bus awaits passengers alighting. Today French's garage runs motor buses, while a respectable pint can yet be enjoyed in the Anchor Inn.

South to Eyemouth, the principal fishing port and coastal town, the cliffs are mainly of red sandstone and of lesser height than those north of St Abbs Head. Fishing is first mentioned at Eyemouth in 1298 when the monastery at Coldingham had among its possessions a 'fishing' within Eyemouth.

No doubt even although this is the earliest written record fishing had been carried out from the mouth of the river Eye since early man first made the most primitive of craft. In the *Statistical Account* of 1791 there are reported only six boats which took, 'an abundance of fishes of all kinds and of a good quality'. Smeaton was busy at the time on a survey of improvements which he considered would enable vessels of up to four hundred tons to use the harbour.

Fishing over the years sometimes concentrated on white fish, bottom dwellers such as cod and haddock being caught by lines. At other times the herring held sway, and were caught on the surface by fleets of nets shot during the hours of darkness. For example, the year after the East Coast Disaster, 1882, was known as the California year, with boats making regular heavy landings of haddock right through until April 1883.

In 1897 it was not uncommon for boats to land 60 boxes of line-caught haddocks, a species for which Eyemouth had a reputation of providing the highest quality. Yet the Rev. Daniel M. Iver states in his book *An Old Time Fishing Town: Eyemouth* published in 1906, that haddock fishing is in decline. 'But alas! Instead of a whole community living upon the product of haddock fishing, there is now only an occasional boat's crew engaged in this almost defunct branch of the fisherman's calling.' For gradually the whole feet gave up the white fishing to follow the migrations of silver herring around the coast. The decline in line fishing was at the time blamed upon the introduction of steam trawling cited as destroying both spawn and young fish. Again from *An Old Time Fishing Town*: 'It is not over-fishing that put an end to the local trade in haddocks; but it was the destructive fishing of the trawlers.'

It could well be said that the argument still rages to this day as fishermen try to cope with EEC quotas of the Total Allowable Catch, which they are be allowed to pursue. Gone are the days when the skipper put to sea with one thought in mind — to catch the maximum possible number of fish in the minimum of

Eyemouth harbour is cramped for modern boats

time, return to port to land and sell that catch, and then return
to sea to repeat the operation. Today there are log books to fill
in with a record of species caught, ready in case the boat should
be boarded by a fisheries patrol, and for a mandatory period be
tied up in port according to size and horsepower.

Eyemouth was once famed for its fleet of seine net boats
which pursued this method of fishing almost to the exclusion
of all others. Seine netting became popular between the World
Wars as it removed much of the drudgery from the lives of
the fisherman's family in the eternal work of bait collection,
line clearing or redding and baiting and coiling the haddock
lines. Seine netting is still pursued fulltime by several larger
Eyemouth based vessels working offshore, but for the smaller
inshore boats it is now only taken up when conditions are
suitable, and mainly in the summer months.

There is little to distinguish between the seine net boat and
the light trawler. Indeed some boats pursue both methods,
while others began life as seine netters before converting to

trawling. Once the main indicator of seine netting was found in the coils of rope piled on the boat's deck, laid down in precise coils by a machine prior to stowing by the crew. This has been surpassed by rope drums or reels, which wind the rope in even coils along the reel's axis. Because of this arrangement fewer crew are required since previously one or two members would be fully engaged in stowing the rope.

To the layman seine netting would appear to be most unlikely method of fish capture. First a flag or dahn is dropped away, then anything up to 12 by 120 fathom coils of rope are shot away in a semicircle. Here the net is placed overboard followed by the same length of rope back to the flag.

With both ends of rope attached to a winch the hauling operation begins, at first slowly, as the rope spurting up mud or sand herds bottom-feeding fish inwards. Speed is gradually increased until the ropes are pointing at the net, when the boat is steamed ahead and the final coils of rope are hauled to the surface.

The operation of setting and hauling a seine net, a shot, only takes around an hour, against a three-to four-hour period when trawling. Fish taken by seine net are usually considered to be of better quality, mainly due to the shorter period spent crushed in the cod end, as the netting bag which holds the catch is called.

Eyemouth's inshore fleet today derives much of its earnings from nephrops or norway lobsters (scampi), known universally as prawns along the entire east coast of Scotland. These are caught by trawling over the muddy sea bed (or ground in fisherman's terms), where the prawn lives in burrows at varying depths.

Prawn trawlers, like the light trawlers for white fish, mainly work day trips, returning to port to land their catch in the evening, or fish nights for prawns during the summer to maximise on the time when nephrops are most easily caught in the grey of dusk and dawn. In the latter case boats will sail in the evening, returning to land in the early hours of the morning. Hence many summer visitors wonder why part of the fleet remains tied up in harbour during daytime when the weather is obviously fine.

Larger vessels in the Eyemouth fleet may sail on Sunday evening, returning to land their catch for overlanding to

Grimsby or Newhaven fishmarkets sometime on Wednesday. Other boats work anything up to ten-day cycles. Known as 'trips' these outings may be to the Norwegian sector of the North Sea, into Shetland waters or west to Rockall in the Atlantic. At least one of the larger vessels owned locally is too big for the harbour and like others of her class is to be found mainly working from ports in the north east of Scotland.

Fishermen and the Eyemouth Harbour Trust have been aware since the 1970s that as the size of the fleet and individual vessels in it had grown the port facilities were becoming inadequate. Plans for a new harbour complex seaward and to the south side of the existing harbour are before the Government at the moment.

The scheme has an estimated cost of over £17 million and a grant from the Scottish Office has been obtained to cover 80 percent of a survey cost. Mr David Dougal, chairman of the harbour trustees, emphasises that this is no guarantee that any actual work may go ahead, but is at least a step in the right direction.

As the major port between Tyne and Forth, Eyemouth provides an important base for vessels, not only from Berwickshire but also from Lothian and Northumbrian ports. Major refurbishmnet schemes have over the past decade been undertaken along Harbour Road, turning derelict property into usefully amenities, such as the net mending hall and fishermen's stores at Meeks yard. A one-time warehouse is now a Mission Centre for the Royal National Mission to Deep Sea Fishermen and opened by 'Take the High Road' actress Eileen Macallum. The canteen there is usually open to the public.

Boat building and repair with engineering facilities are available, together with the services electronic engineers. Electronics, compact and streamlined, following the invention of the transistor and chip, are essential tools for the modern skipper.

Echo sounders chart the nature of the sea bed on colour television screens, revealing the size and nature of shoals and species in different colours. Navigators receive signals from either shore transmitters or satellites, and transfer those if required to plotters, which allow a precise track to be taken

Eileen Macallum actress from 'Take the High Road' opens the R.N.M.D.S.F. at Eyemouth

over any section of the sea bed, while radar bouncing its own transmitted signal from solid objects gives safe passage even in dense fog. The modern deep water trawler is, if nothing else, 'hightech'.

Fish landed from boats working on a daily basis is sold by auction at an evening sale conducted within the covered market at Harbour Road. Buyers comprise mainly fishmerchants, or cadgers as they are known locally, who prepare fish for sale to the public either through retail outlets or van 'fishrounds'. Most of the buyers on Eyemouth market are local but include fishmerchants from the Lothians and south of the Border. At Eyemouth only one firm is engaged in large-scale processing of fish with supplies usually coming from outwith the port.

Shellfish such as crabs and prawns are processed locally, with these species mainly sold under contract terms rather than by auction. Lobsters from the Berwickshire ports, Northumbria and East Lothian, are bought from fishermen by three Eyemouth merchants. Here they are held alive in storage tanks or ponds before consigning to either English markets or to outlets on the Continent.

Eyemouth's summer festival is, not surprisingly, centred around the sea and fishing. 'Herring Queen Week' is held in mid-July, the exact week varying from year to year, to obtain suitable tidal conditions in the harbour. Originated as a peace picnic the crowning of the Herring Queen is one of the most colourful ceremonies of the summer festival calendars. Herring Queen Week is very much a week for the young, the Herring Queen and her Court being elected from the third-year pupils at Eyemouth High School. Saturday is the big day when the Queen and her attendants arrive by boat from St Abbs for the ceremony, escorted by many of the boats in the Eyemouth fleet with pennants flying and rigged with bunting for this unique event.

Finally the Eyemouth Lifeboat escorts the boat chosen to carry the Herring Queen into the harbour to a salvo of rockets fired from the Fort Point and from escorting vessels. After the Queen has been disembarked below Gunsgreen House, a procession, including last year's queen, posy girls and officials, makes its way to a crowning dias near the old lifeboat shed.

The Crowning Ceremony is followed by an oration by a guest speaker and presentations to the Herring Queen, before she herself presents trophies to the boats from the local fleet who have done well in their respective fishings over the past year. A car procession led by Eyemouth Pipe Band tours the town, stopping to lay wreaths at both the war memorial and that commemorating the fishermen who lost their lives in the 1881 disaster.

More than any other outdoor calling that of the fishing industry is at the total mercy of weather conditions. For the seaman this of course means wind, its speed and direction. Modern weather forecasting can do much to warn fishermen of changing conditions while they are at sea, but this was not always the case as a memorial in the old churchyard opening from Eyemouth's High Street records.

On this memorial are the names of the men from the town who lost their lives in one of the most furious storms ever to strike the east coast, when between Newhaven in the Forth and Burnmouth a mile to the south of Eyemouth 189 fishermen lost their lifes, 129 of them from Eyemouth alone.

Friday 14 October 1881 is still known as the 'Disaster Day' when twenty vessels of the Eyemouth fleet were lost, some almost within reach of land. Many in fact were swamped as they tried to regain harbours, and boats which had stood out to sea weathered the storm, although in some cases men were lost overboard.

Despite the extremely low reading on the public weather-glass that morning of 28.451 ins, with bad weather for the previous week confining boats in port, crews were anxious to get to sea. This was morning when conditions were described as a glorious combination of sun and calm with never a whisper of wind or cloud to break the deep blue October sky. A sight as the fleet left Eyemouth Bay and the protection of the Hurkur Rocks described by a landsman as, 'How beautifully close together'. Which drew the retort from an old fisherman, 'Aye! but they'll no be sae close thegither when they come hame.' Three-and-a half hours later the change was sudden from calm and cloudness to first what light wind there was falling calm with an ominous quiet falling over the land. Next the sky darkened and within minutes the sea surface which had been previously unruffled was whipped into a violent maelstrom of foam and flying water.

On the land trees were uprooted to be blown along in an upright position; telegraph wires were cut, while at sea masts were blown away as the boats, some of which were 50ft in length, were lifted clean from the water. Yet there were amazing escapes as some vessels safely passed the Hurkur Rocks and made safe haven. Others were overwhelmed within yards of the shore where would-be rescuers were powerless to lend assistance, such was the severity of the storm.

There were amazing escapes, such as the *Pilgrim*, thrown first on the rocks below Fort Point where a following breaker carried her over Black Carr almost high and dry ashore, where the crew were rescued with the aid of lines. Others of the fleet stood out to sea, not making landfall until the following day. Several boats were driven south to North Shields while the *Progress* from Burnmouth was towed into Bridlington harbour by the gunboat *Firm* at 7 pm on Saturday, 15 October.

A tapestry embroidered by local women records the men and boats lost in 'The Disaster' can be seen in the Eyemouth

Museum at Manse Road. Eyemouth Town Trail includes a visit to the museum, taking the walker around the harbour area with explanation plaques at key points relating to the fishing industry and associated trades such as boat building.

Rapid changes of sea conditions such as those which resulted in the tragic events of 14 October 1881 are seldom so sudden as what took place that day. Usually wind strength increases, or freshens gradually, giving those at sea some warning and time to seek shelter before conditions deteriorate to danger level.

It is worth noting that on the afternoon of 6 October 1990 at around 4 pm the 1881 circumstances of rapid change from calm to storm were encountered. That day the wind had begun as light south east at daybreak, veering to strong westerly at mid-day before falling calm. It was as if someone had flicked a switch as the wind accompanied by horizontal driving rain blasted through from the north-east. Upon the flat calm sea conditions the effect was almost immediate, transforming within minutes the mirror surface where a bath tub would have floated with perfect safety into a vicious maelstrom of thirty-foot waves and wind-driven spume.

Into these desperate conditions sailed the *Eyemouth* lifeboat in response to the maroons fired to alert the crew. Being late Saturday afternoon few fishing vessels were at sea. Numerous diving parties were however both on shore dives and on inflatable boats. Normally the entrance to Eyemouth Harbour would have been impassable, yet under the command of James Dougal, the deputy mechanic who had assumed the position of coxswain in the absence of the first and second cox, the *Eyemouth* Lifeboat battered her way clear of the harbour and the offshore Hurkur Rocks.

Some diving boats did manage to reach harbour under their own power, while others were washed ashore clean over outlying rocks. Meantime helicopters were lifting divers from exposed reefs ashore, while after an hour's search *Eyemouth* lifeboat picked up two of the four missing divers. Dunbar lifeboat, which must have had an unenviable voyage down the Firth of Forth and around St Abbs Head, also joined the search, along with two helicopters from RAF Boulmer in Northumberland.

The crew of Eyemouth lifeboat and Sir John Swinton on the occasion of the presentation of awards

As darkness fell it seemed that the search would now be in vain for the two missing divers. It seemed pointless to continue with the search with both lifeboats being forced to enter Burnmouth harbour, as the entrance to Eyemouth harbour was by this time impassable.

There seemed little chance of survival for the missing pair yet when one of the divers already ashore went to recover gear from his boat below Northburn Caravan Site emergency whistles were heard blowing from seaward. Coastguards were alerted and eventually the missing pair were brought to land safely in what was a truly remarkable escape and an equally remarkable service by the two lifeboat crews. In recognition of the service the RNLBI awarded their silver medal to assistant mechanic James Dougal who was acting coxswain, the Institutions thanks inscribed on vellum going to the crew, and similar thanks being awarded to the crew of the Dunbar lifeboat.

As the modern fisherman must adhere to rules and regulations on his nets and the amount of fish he is allowed to take, his predecessor in the 1850s had also laws to abide by.

Tithes from which the church and parish school received their funding had been paid by each *Eyemouth* vessel up until 1843, which brought a change in the ecclesiastical life throughout Scotland.

Following the Disruption not all children were educated by the parish school, the Free Church of Scotland having also established a school in the town. Feelings which had run high for a number of years erupted, with burning tar barrels being rolled through the streets, effigies being burnt and three local men sent for trial at Duns.

The struggle to abolish tithes lasted until 1863 with demonstrations of 4,000 strong led by the town band parading around the countryside reaching a climax in 1858 with the arrest of fishermen's leader William Spears. Sixteen policemen attempted the arrest of William Spears from his home but unfortunately the alarm was raised as the town rose to his rescue.

Eventually through borrowing, a lump sum in lieu of tithes was raised by the fishermen. This loan was paid off by the fishermen through a weekly levy on the boats ranging from 3s 6d to £1 during the summer herring season.

One of the most recent battles against Authority along the coastal strip was the salmon war of the 1970s around the same time that the 'cod war' was taking place between Britain and Iceland. While the Government had earlier banned the use of drift nets for taking salmon in Scotland, fishermen along the Berwickshire coast managed to find for a time, a legal method employing drift nets to exploit a free swimming fish, which they considered they had every right to catch.

Salmon drift nets are composed of a single transparent strand, monofilament, and despite being described as deadly and invisible, are ineffective in calm conditions when fish are quite capable of avoiding them.

A hard fought battle with an intelligence service to rival a spy thriller operated from the Firth of Forth, reporting mile by mile the progress of fishery patrols leaving their Rosyth base. Likewise the patrols run by the River Tweed Commissioners' Baliff Force from Berwick on Tweed usually arrived at the scene of an alleged crime to find any boats present going about their lawful business.

Tempers became short as the fishermen seemed to be winning the war on sea if not the propaganda through the press:

Frustrated angry were the bailies,
Their feet fair smelly in their wellies,
They scoured aboot an tore their hair,
A case they wanted very sair.

A raid they planned on wee Burnmooth,
Thrae big Eyemooth they held aloof,
The thouchts o sic an easy capture,
It filled the braggarts herts wi rapture.

Eventually hot heads sank the bailiffs' patrol boat at her moorings in the Tweed estuary, and thereafter the full might of HM Navy seemed to be released upon the Berwickshire fleet. Patrol boats and minesweepers (one of the latter, according to local legend, commanded by HR Highness the Prince of Wales), backed up by helicopter patrols, became an everyday occurrence.

Fishermen in fact said that if in need of rescue there was no need to fire rockets or send out mayday calls. Merely dropping a few yards of salmon drift net overboard would speedily bring navy patrols and helicopters to rescue and arrest.

Despite the crew of one Fisheries Patrol boat eating the evidence in the shape of a prime salmon taken from a net, the forces of the Establishment prevailed in the end. Where patrols from the sea could always be anticipated, there was no protection from airborne surveillance. Fines up to £2,000, plus the growing number of farmed salmon keeping the price of wild fish low, with legislation blocking the loophole previously exploited, finally persuaded fishermen that salmon catching was for them not an economical business.

The matter still rankles. Since the inshore industry is going through a lean time there is a feeling that a limited salmon fishery properly run could be sustained along the coastline. Berwickshire District Council have in fact sought to establish such a fishery but there at the moment the matter rests.

Prior to the early 1900s Eyemouth had the reputation of being a smugglers haven where large imports of duty-free tobacco, spirits and tea were made. Throughout the old town of the time the maze of wynds and back lanes was well suited to the evader of customs officers. Even Gunsgreen House, the showpiece on the harbour, is, according to tradition, riddled with secret tunnels and doors, designed to facilitate the storage of contraband and the escape of the smugglers.

Despite what must have been a hatred for men of that calling Scotland's most famous exciseman, Robert Burns, was made a Royal Arch Mason at Eyemouth.

South from Eyemouth, where the south bank of the river Eye marks the start of the golf course, where the old mansion house of Gunsgreen is now the clubhouse, the coastline rises in steps to the lofty heights of Hawks Ness before dropping to the village of Lower Burnmouth — or rather the three villages 'doon the brae' which bear the collective name.

Partanhall, Cowdrait and Ross make up the lower village, although few fishermen now live at the foot of the steep hill from upper village. Somewhat isolated from any of the houses, Burnmouth Harbour, although tidal, offers a safe haven for fishing vessels when other ports on the east coast cannot be entered due to heavy swell.

Sheltered from the north and north-east by outlying skeers and carrs boats may enter Burnmouth when seas are breaking within the harbour entrance of other ports. Today the boats fishing from Burnmouth concentrate mainly upon crabs and lobsters. Larger vessels owned by Burnmouth fishermen now operate from Eyemouth, although within recent memory seine net boats fished from Burnmouth.

South from Burnmouth, where Ross is the most southerly of the villages, the cliffs are formed of sandstone much sculpted by nature into curious shapes and forms. Wind-blown spray, the action of wave and water have over eons cut and gouged the rock, first creating then destroying returning sandstone to sand leaving for a short span something of beauty.

Clinging to a narrow platform above the cliffs and below the Moors of Lamberton run the main east coast railway and the A1 road. So close is the railway that the passenger looking from a carriage window seems to peer straight down to the rocky beaches which are a feature of this part of the coastline. Sea erosion in fact required considerable civil engineering in the mid-1980s when the line was threatened with undermining and landslide.

The remains of an old salmon netting station are to be found at Lumburn where a ruined shiel stands above the rocky shelving beach, still with its hand winches used for hauling nets. Finally the Borders coastline ends at a low stone dyke at Lamberton, the march with Northumbria, the Bounds of Berwick and England. Beside the A1 once stood Lamberton Toll, as notorious for runaway weddings in its time as the famous Gretna Green. Now demolished, nothing marks the Border here today other than the road signs indicating change of Country, Region and District.

Plans have been mooted over the years for a tourist complex on the Border to replace the old Toll House at Lamberton, but as yet no sod has been cut on this project. Just north of the Border where the old A1 curves inland a branch road leads west to Lamberton. Here overlooking the sea are the ruins of Lamberton Kirk with a tiny burial ground. This is where a ceremony between James IV and Princess Margaret of England took place in 1503. Some accounts give this as a marriage, others a betrothal ceremony; Wilson's *Tales of the Borders* enlarges the event into a grand affair.

Wilson sets a grand scene with great festivities, sports, feasting, the full works. King James himself arrived incognito, determined to take an active part in the pre-nuptial celebrations. Wrestling is one of the sports where James is engaged in a bout with a young fisherman known as Strong Andrew. The match over, Andrew and James take a shine to one another, with the former inviting the king, who he does not know as such, home for a bite and sup. Andrew's mother is preparing fish, but not enough it seems for her son's and the King's appetite. 'Gut three, wuman, gut three' says Andrew, leading James to declare that from now Andrew is to be known as Guthree or Guthrie, a fairly common name in Berwickshire.

Below, on the beach, the boundary between Scotland and England, Scotland and The Liberties of Berwick and Berwickshire and Northumbria are marked by a low dry stone wall, where we must leave the coast to discover the hinterland of The Merse.

# CHAPTER 3

## *The Merse*

Snugged into the south-east corner of Scotland the Merse is perhaps not regarded as Borderland compared to further west in Tweed and Teviotdale. Known as the Eastern March prior to the Union of the Crowns the Merse lacks the imagined 'romance' of the riever country Middle March, yet here was every bit a frontier, often first to bear the brunt of the ambitious expansionist southorn.

Armies marching north from Tynedale were forced east by the Cheviots, only crossed otherwise by hill tracks, which if Dere Street or Gamel's Path as it is also called, is discounted, are unsuited for the movement of large forces. Dere Street was not the only road used by the Romans between Tyne and Tweed as the course of the 'Devil's Causeway' is shown running up the north Northumberland coastal plain right to the outskirts of Berwick. As did the Romans, so would the later forces from the time of the Scottish Independence Wars right up until the Union of Crowns.

Taking the coastal route made a natural choice for army commanders through the ages, provisioning from the sea an attractive option in a time of poor roads, and furthermore in the face of a populace who would rather burn their homes and crops than allow an invader to use them.

The first bridge over the Tweed estuary at Berwick is said to have existed in the time of Malcolm IV of Scotland, it and its replacements being subject to destruction by floods. However, the strategic importance of the town from the twelfth century onwards ensured that it was the first port of call for any invader. Fords at Ladykirk and Coldstream, with the riches of the Merse within easy reach, meant that even if the sixteenth-century cattle lifting bands were less active here, invasion and organised pillage were still to the fore.

Several definitions of the area covered by the Merse and its use as place name a name for this part of Scotland can be considered. The Rev. Walter Anderson of Chirnside, writing in

56

the *Statistical Account for Scotland* gives us one version, 'Chirnside is the name of a considerable village and parish, in the shire of Berwick, vulgarly called the Merse, but, more properly, the March, upon the E. border of Scotland.' Here then is one source in march for boundary; it remains a term in regular usage. The Berwickshire born and bred farmer will refer to his 'march' — dyke — fence — hedge — his property in fact marches with his neighbour's.

The term merse is also applied to flat alluvial land found around the shores of the Solway Firth, where it is landscape description. While this would not describe the configuration of the east March, it could apply to the conditions underfoot as marsh, before fens and mires were drained. A print of a map of eastern Berwickshire, 'Mercia' from the coast west to Coldstream is dated 1645, while the Anglian kingdom of Mercia was not too far distant.

The area covered by Merse has through the years been subjected to some alteration. Referring here again to the *Statistical Account for Scotland*, the Duns Minister, Rev. Robert Bowmaker has this to say, 'The Merse is that part of the country, which is bounded by the river Tweed on S. and S. E., by part of Tiviotdale and Lauderdale on the S. and S. W. and by the Lammermoor hills on the N. W. and N. with the town of Berwick at the East point. It is a plain of at least 25 miles from E. to W. and takes the name of Merse from being a border county.'

What is described here is Berwickshire, prior to the county status being swept aside in the local government re-organisation in the mid-1970s, the Rev. Bowmaker endorsing the meaning of the word as a border or boundary.

In the modern Merse landscape the presence of protected dwellings from castle to fortified house are not immediately obvious. Yet they are and were here, spread out and scattered rather than concentrated alongside the river valleys as, for example, those of Teviot and Yarrow.

Berwick, castle and town, were as often in English as in Scottish hands, as were Roxburgh and Jedburgh. Truly English castles at Norham and Wark immediately south of the Tweed were always a further threat needing the appropriate precautions by at least those who could afford such protection.

Duns Castle the earliest part on the right dates from 1320

Original towers and peels are hidden within the fabric of some present-day houses; others have been completely replaced by later more comfortable buildings on the same sites. Farm steadings may have part of an old keep whole within their walls, or more likely an adjacent tower used as a convenient quarry. Of others, grassy mounds, a few fragments of stonework, or even only a place name marks the passing of peel and castle.

Three castles once formed a defensive chain along the southern edge of the Lammermuirs:

> Bunkle, Billie and Blanerne
> Three castles strong as airn
> Built when Davy was a bairn
> They'll a gang doon
> Wi Scotland's croon
> And ilka ane shall be a cairn.

Of these strongholds other than Blanerne, little remains but a few scraps of stonework amid green mounds. Bunkle can be seen beside the Reston to Duns road where the nearby church is also worth a visit. The small building on the south side of the present church is the remains of the pre-Reformation church — an excellent example of Scottish medieval architecture.

Billie Castle, once guardian of a vital pass through Billiemire, displays today little of its past importance. Billiemire is a pleasant excursion by path and track from the centre of the village of Auchencrow or Edincraw, the old name still used locally.

Edrington Castle shares the same fate as Bunkle and Billie, while at Ayton and Wedderburn, once under the command of the Home family, modern mock castles occupy the sites. Within the Merse, Duns Castle, where the oldest part of the building dates from the fourteenth century, is the best remaining example of a defensive house in Berwickshire.

Well preserved and renovated towers exist at Cranshaws in the Lammermuirs and Purves Hall beside the Coldstream Greenlaw road, but like Duns Castle are not normally open to the public. Of other Merse 'castle' remains it is difficult to distinguish from their paltry ruins the difference between their Ordnance Survey description as a Tower at the village of Leitholm and the Bastle near Printonan farm.

Travellers on the A1 see little of the Merse, the view being blocked by the bulk of Lamberton Moors, and then enclosed by the valleys of the river Eye and Pease Burn. Those entering over the river Tweed at Coldstream pass through the heartland, where from here north to Greenlaw it would be easy to dismiss this area as a boring progression of acre upon acre of cereal crops. The treasures must be sought, the river valleys of Blackadder and Whiteadder, the great houses and the country kirks surrounded by the stones marking the passing of those who have created this land over the centuries.

Despite the implications of Merse as flat boggy ground the landscape of old central Berwickshire County is far from flat and level. Although within are found sites of two World War II airfields at Charterhall and Winfield, these level areas are an exception. Rather for the most part the landscape rises, dips and rises again from the Tweed basin up to the Lammermuirs.

Towns, villages and farms for the most part are sited on the ridges, an indication perhaps that the original choice of settlements was due to the unsuitability of the lower hollows. These ridges are partly the result of the retreating Tweed glacier depositing fluvio-glacial debris into, 'drumlin swarm' or drumlin field — whaleback mounds. Below in places are rich clay marls once exploited as an early form of fertiliser.

It is upon the banks of the Tweed that events thrust the Merse firmly into Border country, following the Northumbrians defeat at Carham in 1018 by Malcolm II of Scotland, establishing the Tweed as a national boundary. Across the river at Birgham a treaty in 1290 is supposed to have ratified this Border, but in fact laid the way open for King Edward I of England to play a meddlesome part in Scottish affairs.

The Treaty of Birgham arranged a marriage between Princess Margaret of Norway, grand-daughter of Alexander III and heiress to the Scottish crown to the son of Edward I, which would have paved the way to a union of crowns over three hundred years before that event took place. Had the Princess not died in Orkney on the way south the course of history between Scotland and England might have been greatly changed. More than anything else the soils of the Merse are famed for their agricultural produce. Toil and sweat of generations of farmers and their workers have shaped the modern landscape, converting sour bog and marsh to sweet fertile soil. Back in the mists of time it must have been discovered that here were ideal circumstances for growing grain crops. Indeed Berwick or Barwick means barley town, as true today as at any time down the centuries. An example of what the land was once like in the Parish of Swinton, as central to the Merse as anywhere, can be gauged from the writing of the Rev. George Cupples in 1791–2 in *The Statistical Account of Scotland*:

> From some undrained marshy grounds, from some low lying spots which long retain the waters in a stagnated state, the air is often moist, foggy, and seemingly unwholesome, though so much so as one would conclude, the inhabitants living as long, and enjoying as much health as in other places; except that there is one disease very prevalent, namely the ague, the cause of which seems to be the miry nature of the ground, the fogginess of the air, the defect of in cleanliness, and the scanty portion of animal food which falls to their share.

Sheep are one of the most labour intensive 'crops' John and Bill Kerr Darnchester West Mains

Cereals remain the principle crop throughout the Merse with an emphasis on high-quality malting barley and milling wheat. Maltings on Tweedmouth Trading Estate at Berwick convert barley into malt for either home based or overseas distillers and brewers. Cereals may be the main crop for Berwickshire farmers but these are by no means a monoculture grown to the exclusion of all others.

Oilseed rape and fodder peas are also exported, but added to these can be root crops, potatoes with the swede grown for stock feed or through a local firm prepacked for human consumption. Lifting swedes finds large gangs at work as machinery is unable to harvest turnips to the quality required for supermarket shelves. Potato harvesting is becoming more exclusively undertaken by machine every year; the rows of bent human forms scrabbling behind the potato digger being now almost a scene of the past.

Writing in *Coldingham Priory and Parish*, published in 1908, J. P. F. Bell records the principal range of crops as, 'oats, barley, wheat, hay, peas, beans, turnips, mangel-worzel, potatoes, rye

and flax — the two latter in very small areas'. Yields and quality
he describes in the lands near the coast as being excellent at
an average of six quarters to the acre, weighing in at four
pounds per bushel. In the early 1970s when the Scottish sugar
beet factory at Cupar Angus was closed, Berwickshire farmers
were forced to look elsewhere for a suitable break crop. This
brought vegetable growing into serious consideration, resulting
in the formation of the East Lothian and Borders Growers
Association and the construction of a processing and freezing
plant at Eyemouth, now run by Christian Salvesen.

Originally peas were, in fact they still are, one of the main
crops, the convoy of pea harvests and their back up team
working day and night to catch this crop in peak condition for
freezing. Beans and courgettes are other crops of the summer
season backed up in winter by carrots, turnips and brassica, such
as sprouts and cauliflower.

At the same time as vegetable growing was established
some farmers began growing soft fruits. These are on a
pick-your-own basis and supply to retail and wholesale outlets.
Strawberries, raspberries, black and red currants are the main
crop, plus a few tayberries and logan berries.

Although declined somewhat stock husbandry remains an
important aspect of farming in this part of the world. Beef
cattle are still fattened indoors over the winter months, while
sheep are not restricted to the slopes of the Lammermuirs or
Cheviots, but not unnaturally most sheep farming takes place
in the upland areas. Fortunately the farmers of Berwickshire
have not adopted the one field one farm ideology, massacring
field boundaries and hedgerows in the name of progress. True,
some hedges have been lost, but the patchwork of fields remains
here, to a great extent providing the shelter essential for stock
and crops.

What has gone are the workers. Machinery has replaced
the labour of generations of farm workers who followed
the plough or drove the early slow low-powered tractors.
Farms which once supported ten families may today have
only one or two workers, or even be run entirely by the
farmer's family. Gone are the days when the farm workers'
terms or contract required the provision of a female farm
servant, 'a bondager' to work in the fields as required. Even

Pick your own at Blackhouse near Reston

up to thirty years ago farm job vacancies would include such provisios as, 'must have son to assist/ dairyman/ cattleman/ shepherd, etc.'

Increasingly most of the work at peak periods is undertaken by contractors moving from farm to farm to cultivate — sow — spray — then harvest as the season dictates. This has naturally had an effect on the rural population as the displaced workers have moved from the land into towns and villages.

In the Merse as elsewhere the modern farm worker has a lonely job, enclosed in a solitary machine capable of carrying out in one pass over the land what once required the labour of five men. Gone may be the hard physical toil, much of it dirty, boring and unpleasant, replaced by the urgency which was always there of seedtime and harvest cast now upon fewer shoulders.

Village schools, shops and churches have closed, the once prolific provision vans of the baker, butcher and grocer have all but vanished as the remaining car owning population seek their weekly needs elsewhere. Not that the drift from the land is anything new, as the trend began with the enclosure of land in the eighteenth century, when the old runrig system was abandoned. Horses replaced oxen and better ploughs required fewer ploughmen to work the same acreage; each new invention has accelerated the trend.

What certainly does not apply to the modern farm worker is the term labourer. In charge of machinery valued at thousands of pounds, making precise measurements of the chemical compounds, to name but a few, the term technician would be a more apt description today. Wages are now in cash but it is only recently that the custom of receiving part payment in kind in the shape of a ton of potatoes has fallen into disuse.

It was a Berwickshire man, James Small, who assisted an early agricultural revolution with the invention of the chain plough, sometimes referred to as the 'English plough', but Small was brought up in the Merse, being assisted in his early endeavours by Lord Kames.

To view these wide farming acres stretching down from the foothills of the Lammermuirs to the Tweed, rising beyond

Hume Castle, currently this shell is being renovated by The Berwickshire Civic Society

towards the Cheviots, a better vantage point than Hume Castle would be difficult to find.

Impressive as it may be from a distance, Hume Castle is an empty shell, a folly raised from the ruins of the original Home stronghold by the third Earl of Marchmont. Hume derives from *Hom* in the Celtic language or *Holm* in Saxon, both of which signify a hill, which is very true of Hume, the most prominent feature of the Merse.

Hume was the principal fortress of the Home family who over the years played a major part in the politics of Scotland and had arrived at Hume around AD 1225. The Home history begins around this period when William son of Waldeave, 4th Earl of Dunbar, married his cousin Ada about that time, through her acquiring the Barony and lands of Hume — assuming the name William de Hume, i.e., William of the Hill. The first title, that of Lord Home, was conferred on Sir Alexander Home when he was made Lord of Parliament by King James III in 1473. The Barony and lands of Hume were bestowed on the 3rd Lord Home in 1509 by James IV,

the 6th Lord Home being created Earl of Home by James VI
in 1605.

The Homes were very active in Scottish affairs: two were
Priors of Coldingham, two Great Chamberlains of Scotland,
one Keeper of Edinburgh Castle, one a Prioress of Abbey
St Bathans, one ambassador to England and Spain, and one
a Privy Councillor, and of course Wardens of the East March.
Following the death of James IV at Flodden the 3rd Lord
Home, Alexander, and his brother William became embroiled
in the political intrigue pursued by the factions of the Dowager
Queen Margaret Tudor, Archibald Douglas, 6th Earl of Angus
and James, Duke of Albany, who assumed the Regency upon
Margaret Tudor marrying James Douglas.

It was a time of changing alliances. As the custody of the
young King was hotly disputed, the Homes were the most
unfortunate of the Scottish nobility of the time with both
Alexander and his brother William being executed for treason
in Edinburgh, which was to have later repercussions in the
Merse.

Hume Castle's prominent position and that of the Homes
made it a target for at least two sieges, once in 1547 when Lord
Home had been fatally injured in a skirmish at Prestonpans and
his son taken hostage, Lady Home being forced to surrender to
Somerset Lord Protector of England who installed a garrison of
60 musketeers, 40 horse and a hundred pioneers.

In 1548 the stronghold was retaken, led by an old man of
Home name who scaled the walls at their most difficult but
lightest defended point. Holingshed in the *English Chronicles*
claims that treachery by 'assured' Scots had led to the castle's
downfall. Sussex was back in 1565 laying siege, where after a
short artillery duel the garrison surrender was agreed with Lord
Home who was apparently not within the castle at the time but
lurked nearby. Terms allowed the 168 men of the garrison to
walk free without arms or accoutrements of war.

In 1840, when Britain was alert to Napoleonic invasion, the
entire Borderland was alerted by a false alarm from a beacon
lit in error by the Hume watchman. From crag to crag through
the Borders the warning sped, Sir Walter Scott riding 100 miles
from Cumberland to Dalkeith in 24 hours to take up his military
post.

From Hume is said to originate the children's rhyme 'King of the Castle', coined by a cocksure garrison commander James Cockburn in a taunt to Cromwellian besiegers under George Fenwick.

I Willie Wastle,
Stand firm in my castle,
An a' the dugs in your toon,
Can no ding Willie Wastle doon.

A boast as empty as Hume's shell today, the castle soon fell, its walls ultimately flung down. Hume was once open to the public where an indicator erected by The Berwickshire Naturalists Society pointed the most important landmarks. Now closed because of its dangerous condition the shrouding scaffolding indicates that at least repairs are taking place with access available again some time in the future. At the moment the visitor must be content with the views from the crag encompassing the Borderland and Northumbria.

Readers may note that both the Hume and Home spellings are used. There is always some argument about the spelling and pronunciation, but it is generally accepted that the castle and village are spelt as Hume while the family name is spelt Home, but pronounced as Hume.

Motorists travelling along the A697 may wonder why a small village such as Greenlaw, 'Grinly' in local parlance, can boast what appears to be such a magnificent town hall. This rather splendid building with stone columns and domed roof on the town green served for seventy-five years as the county hall and court for Berwickshire.

Prior to Duns assuming the mantle of county administration in 1904, Greenlaw had held the position of county town since 1598. The Grecian hall was built with financial aid from Sir William Purves Hume Campbell of Marchmont who had originally undertook to pay half the costs. Perhaps the County coffers were at a low ebb as eventually Sir William footed the entire £6,500 for the building.

After being abandoned as county headquarters the hall became the centre of social life in Greenlaw until in the 1950s damp and dry rot began to take their toll upon the

Greenlaw Hall, ex county hall for Berwickshire

fabric. A brave attempt financed by the local community brought a change of use as Berwickshire's first swimming pool in the 1970s. Unfortunately shortly afterwards other pools were built at Duns and Eyemouth, thus making the Greenlaw facility unviable through underuse.

After a period of semi-dereliction the old county hall with its swimming pool floored over is now used by an antiques dealer as a furniture store and display area. What appears to be the spire of Greenlaw Parish Church which stands behind the old county hall is in fact a tower jail dating from 1712. On the west side of the jail once stood the courthouse. The church remains on its east side as is recorded in the rhyme:

> Here's the gospel and the law
> Hell's hole atween the twa.

Once a bastion of the Humes nearby Marchmont House is today a nursing home run by the Sue Ryder foundation, having been purchased for this purpose from the MacEwen family. Sitting in extensive wooded policies Marchmont was the scene of grand

Polwarth Kirk, where Grisel Home secretly brought food to her father who was in hiding in the burial vault

social occasions where guests included members of the Royal Family.

Marchmont House replaced the old Redbraes, made famous, as every Berwickshire primary school child knows, by the story of Grisel Home. Grisel's father, Patrick Home, an ardent covenanter, was in 1684 being sought avidly by troops of King Charles II. So close was the search that Patrick Home had no time to flee the district, being forced to hide in the gloomy burial vault of nearby Polwarth Kirk.

Nightly for over a month Grisel brought what food she could remove by stealth from the family table to her father in this grisly cavern. Secrecy was vital in case young members of the family might let anything slip to the soldiers billeted at Redbraes, leading one of Grisel's brothers to remark that, 'Grisel had eaten a whole sheep's head while the family were at their broth.'

The sheep's head had of course been slipped into concealment by Grisel to be delivered later under cover of darkness to her father in hiding. Patrick Home later escaped to Holland to

return and reclaim his estates when William of Orange became
king.

For many years a strange custom prevailed at Polworth
marriages where the wedding party danced around the
Polworth Thorn tree.

> At Polwart-on-the Green
> Our forebearers oft were seen,
> To dance around the Thorn
> Sae we their like wha be,
> Shall keep the ancient glee
> Nor let the gree gan doon,
> While Polwart is a toun.

The origins of this unusual practice are thought to date from
the time when George and Patrick Home of Wedderburn
courted the sisters Marion and Margaret Sinclair, heiresses to
Polworth and Kimmergame. This wooing did not meet with the
approval of the young ladies' uncle and guardian, Sir William
Sinclair, who removed them to what he thought was the safety
of Herdmanston in the Lammermuirs.

Sir William should have known better, for soon the Home
brothers were galloping around Herdmanston demanding the
release of their prospective brides. Their uncle now found that
discretion was the better part of valour when faced by this
warlike bunch of Merse men led by Wedderburn Homes, and
he turned the girls over to their suitors.

A double wedding was celebrated at Polworth where
the dancing around the Thorn is said to have been a
ceremonial version of Patrick and George Home galloping
around Herdmanston. Dancing around the thorn continued
for many centuries. The tree itself, or a successor of the
original, is now under the watchful eye of the Berwickshire
Civic Trust as some housing development is proposed in its
vicinity.

Lady Grisel Home married George Bailie of Mellerstain
where she and her husband were responsible for the com-
missioning of the present Adam designed mansion house.
Mellerstain is today the home of the Earl and Countess of
Haddington. It is open to the public and administered by the
Mellerstain Charitable Trust.

Mellerstain House

Sheltered from the north, Mellerstain lies in a magnificent setting, the view south reaching over the terraced gardens sweeping down close cropped lawns to an artificial lake and then rising beyond to the rim of the Cheviots. Fine timber, including beeches and limes, surrounds the lake, which makes a pleasant walk from the terraced garden, not forgetting to visit the small fishpond just below the terrace, where the semi-tame carp will suck at a finger placed on the water surface.

Art treasures within the house include paintings by many famous artists, including Gainsborough and Van Dyck, with family portraits. Upstairs the gallery has items of historical interest on display, including Prince Charles Edward Stuart's bagpipes and a letter from Sir Walter Scott.

Of the architectural features inside Mellerstain the most striking are the Adam ceilings with their raised white figures against a background of Wedgwood blue, depicting scenes from classical Greek mythology, including the Nine Muses and the Choice of Hercules.

According to one of the Mellerstain guides Wedgwood was inspired in his pottery by the designs of Adam, these two leading figures in design being at one time all but next-door neighbours in London. Not to be missed in the grounds is the circular thatched cottage straight out of a fairy tale, its walls an excellent example of the harling or roughcasting technique mentioned in an earlier chapter.

Greenknowe Tower, dated 1581, near the village of Gordon, and bearing the initials of James Seaton and Jane Edmonston, is perhaps an example of what homes of Border lairds such as Patrick Hume's Redbraes were like before these towers were replaced by mansions. Nearby is Gordon Moss Wildlife Reserve with its alders and wetland plants, one of the few such remaining marshes in the Merse.

Gordon village has come to prominence in local news with the proposed development of a golf course and hotel complex plus the proposed construction of 250 houses which would in effect double the size of this rather isolated village. As usual there are those for and against such a large-scale development in a rural area which at the time of writing remains in the planning stage.

Returning to Greenlaw after following the fortunes of Grisel Hume who is buried in the grounds of Mellerstain, Hule Moss across the A6105 from Marchmont is an important wintering site for wild geese which spread out from here across the Merse to glean winter pickings.

A short length of earth rampart, 'Heriot's Dyke', its purpose uncertain, but allegedly extended at one time from Berwick-on-Tweed in the east to Ledgerwood in the west, runs for about a mile across Greenlaw Moor for almost a dead straight mile also adjacent to the A6105.

From Greenlaw, as the A697 skirts the edge of the Lammermuirs the village of Westruther nestles around its inn, anciently Wolfstruther. Here is said to be one of the last outposts of wolves in Scotland. Above the Southern Upland Way passes by Twin Law capped by the matching Twinlaw Cairns. These it is said mark the site of an encounter between Saxon and British armies, where instead of an all out battle champions were elected by either side to decide the outcome.

Dick Lauder has the following to say about a poem recording the event:

Greenknowe Tower near Gordon

This contest has been celebrated in a poem, which seems to have escaped the diligence of the collectors of ancient ballads. It does not bear the mark of great antiquity, but has been known in the parish for at least a century and a half. It is given as taken down from the recital of an old inhabitant:

> In days of yore, when deeds were rife,
> And wars on banks and braes,
> And nocht but strife on every side,
> Which brought on dule and waes,
> The Anglo-Saxon's restless band,
> Had crossed the river Tweed;
> Up for the hills of Lammermuir,
> Their hosts marched on with speed.
>
> A chieftain from the Saxon band,
> Exulting in his might,
> Defied the bravest of the Scots,
> To come to single fight.

Girded and helmeted the champions fought until the Saxon fell when it was discovered that unknown to each other twin brothers had fought in single combat where the Saxon warrior was slain. One it seems had been abducted by the Saxon's in infancy and raised as the king's own son:

> An aged Saxon came to view,
> The body of his chief;
> His streaming eyes and downcast looks,
> Bespoke a heart of grief.
>
> 'He's dead,' he cried, 'the bravest youth
> E'er sprang from Edgar's line;
> I bore him from the Scottish coasts,
> And made him pass for mine.'

Old Edgar, the Scottish king, collapses and dies on the spot, while the surviving son tears the bandages from his wounds and bleeds to death.

> He kissed his sire and his brother's wounds,
> That ghastly were and deep,
> And closed him in his folding arms,
> And fell on his long, long sleep.

From Twin Law the Southern Upland Way continues east by the Watch Water Reservoir built in the early 1950s to provide a water supply for Berwickshire. Gravity fed for much of the county connection to 'the Watch' replaced the 'hard' lime rich water drawn from wells and bore holes with the 'soft' peaty water of the uplands.

As water consumption has increased throughout the country bore holes are again being sunk into the old red sandstone layers by the Borders Region to exploit again the underground reservoirs to supplement the Watch resources.

Near Longformacus the Watch Water, the name now meaning stream, enters the larger Dye whose source lies west of the Mutiny Stones on Fallago Ridge. Dye's first tributary flowing between Little and Meikle (Big) Law is unusual in its name 'Burn betwixt the Laws'. The Dye itself joins the larger Whiteadder near Ellemford village where the Southern Upland Way tags along downstream to Abbey St Bathans Village.

A visit to Abbey St Bathans in late spring as the first traces of greenery begin to clothe the tree-clad valley will not bring disappointment. Ample car parking space can be found near the trout farm site which also incorporates a tearoom with several short walks available alongside the River Whiteadder through a natural woodland of stunted oaks.

Christianity first came to this part of the Whiteadder valley sometime in the seventh or eighth century with the establishment of a chapel. Later in the twelfth century a Priory for a community of nuns was founded by Ada, Countess of March, wife of Patrick, 5th Earl of Dunbar. Part of the Priory, said to have measured over 84 feet by 58 feet, is incorporated within the walls of the present church.

Unusual in the church building is the use of round red sandstone columns at the main door and again on the belfry. These make a strong contrast with the blue black semi-dressed whinstone used in much of the fabric. To be seen in the churchyard are a number of carved tombstones depicting figures holding open books, crossed bones, hour glasses and on one a shepherd's crook.

Across the narrow lane from the church a comfortable hostel has been adapted from old buildings to accommodate walkers, with a new bridge over the Whiteadder a few yards distant on the Southern Upland Way having been constructed by the Gurkha Regiment.

Leaving the Whiteadder Valley towards the north-east passersby may wonder at the array of gigantic tyres and apparent tank traps at Whiteburn farm, where is to be found farmer Ronnie Dale's Off-Road Adventure Driving School.

Off-the-road vehicles with four-wheel drive, commonly known as 4 × 4s are for many Borderers, either an essential tool of daily life or used for recreational purposes. Ordinarily it can take months or even years of experience to drive a 4 × 4 safely to its maximum capability. Having himself twice undergone the strenuous instructor training course given by Landrover, plus his own experience, Ronnie can transfer much of this required knowledge to pupils on his day course.

At the 25-acre Whiteburn training area and in nearby forestry using the pupil's own 4 × 4, or one of the school's vehicles, every situation met in practical off-the-road driving can be duplicated. Fun days or corporate entertainment are another feature of the Whiteburn training area, while the facilities are also available for dealers and manufactureres to demonstrate to the best advantage the capabilities of their machines.

On a shelf of land below Cockburn Law itself, crowned by a fort, stands another of Berwickshire's unusual antiquities in the shape of Edin's Hall, described on OS maps as Fort & Broch. Edin's Hall can be reached from the A6112 Duns-Grantshouse road at the junction leading to Abbey St Bathans, or as a designated walk from Abbey St Bathans trout farm where full details are available.

Taking the first-mentioned approach, follow a track through woodland, taking the lower branch where the track forks, leading shortly to an area of open meadow beside the river Whiteadder. Despite the dire notice saying it is dangerous, cross the suspension bridge, then follow the way markers first upstream, then uphill to the Broch. Edin's Hall, the most southerly of the Pictish Brochs, consists of a circular walled area not unlike a sheep stell standing some six feet in height. Walls are of double thickness enclosing a number of chambers and what were possibly 'sentry boxes' at the gateway.

Returning to the suspension bridge, downstream on the north bank are the entrances to the old copper mines — an

Edins Hall Broch on a shoulder of Cockburn Law

unusual glimpse of industry in this remote location. At first the ore appeared to be promising but soon ceased to be economical and was soon abandoned.

This area seems to have been popular with early man even long before Edin built his residence above the Whiteadder. Downstream on the opposite bank a haugh on the farm of Hoardweel frequently yields up small stone tools and arrow heads. According to Wilson Hoardweel was the scene of the discovery of a remarkable gold chain, but remember Wilson's literary pedigree from the previous chapter.

The circumstances were that a farm worker had taken a piece of machinery, most likely a plough, to be repaired at the local blacksmiths. As no new material was available to make this repair it was suggested that the job could be completed by using a piece of mud encrusted chain which had been found at Hoardweel some time previously. This was started but when the smith cut through the dirt the chain was found to be of solid gold, an apparent method in ancient times used to conceal valuable metals.

Beside the Whiteadder a short distance from Duns only the mill part of the name Cumledge Mill marks the site of the only large-scale woollen industry ever located in the Merse. Once every Berwickshire bride could expect a pair of Cumledge blankets famed for their quality among her wedding presents. Changing fashions in bedding to continental duvets brought the demise of Cumledge Mill in the 1960s, the mill itself being demolished, while the workers houses were converted into upmarket dwellings.

With such fertile agriculture land forestry on a large scale is not a feature in the lower part of the Merse. Plantations usually mean estate rather than farming ownership although there are exceptions. Hardwoods, beech, oak and sycamore are often there simply because of the sheer beauty of deciduous trees the year round. Ultimately of course they face the chain saw, but they are a long-term theme rather than a commercial crop.

A change is afoot on some lower ground estates as reduction in grant aid hits the profitability of farming as the main source of income. More and more can be seen small plantations of hardwoods on prime agricultural land which up until the 1990s would have been unthinkable.

Away from the low ground it is in the Lammermuirs where commercial timber growing in the shape of softwoods is carried out to a greater extent. As yet the blanket of afforestation as seen in the upper Tweed basin has not occurred on the Lammermuirs within Berwickshire. The largest recent block of softwoods within the old county boundary, measuring around $2\frac{1}{2} \times 1\frac{1}{2}$ miles is found at Dunter Law.

Conifers such as sitka spruce and scots pine are no newcomer to the slopes of the Lammermuirs; a long-established plantation can be seen on Duns Castle Estate north from Duns Law. Once softwood went for local use such as fencing and hurdle making. Today a large proportion may go for pulp and chipboard or may be used for local manufacture into storage pallets for industry.

Woodland in the Merse is often there for purposes other than timber production. Amid the Lammermuirs woodland takes the form of shelterbelts to provide a lee for stock when winds sweep through the cleughs and glens.

Shooting is now an important consideration for many landowners, not only in the Merse, but throughout the Borders. Grouse shooting in the Lammermuirs is considered some of the best in the country, which, like the woodland pheasant shooting, draws an increasing number of visitors from Britain, Europe and America to test their skills against driven grouse and pheasant. Farms coming on the market in this decade of the 1990s are often purchased as much for their sporting as their farming potential.

Other than farming most employment within the Merse is in service industries, the building trade and engineering. Even here much of this is directed towards the agriculture industry in some form or another. Cereal complexes provide further jobs in drying and storing grain for export with naturally a seasonal peak around harvest time.

Manufacturing on a large scale only takes place at Chirnside where the Dexter Corporation of America operate the papermill producing 'non-wovens', e.g. tea bags, to name one product. The Dexter operation brought a huge expansion for Chirnside and the surrounding area with the then Berwickshire County Council building a complete new housing estate for the workers.

Ninewells on the haugh below the Chirnside was the home of the famous philosopher David Hume, like the rest of the present Home family is pronounced as Hume, the spelling adopted by the philosopher for his own name.

Hume held a number of important positions on the international scene having been aide-de-campe to the Embassies of Turin and Vienna and secretary to the Paris Ambassador. His last work, written at the age of sixty four, when he suffered from an incurable illness, records his life and ambitions from his earliest days at Ninewells.

A monument in Chirnside churchyard records the adherence to the principles of Henry Erskine, minister here in the latter half of the seventeenth century. Removed from his charge at Cornhill in Northumberland Erskine served periods of imprisonment, including incarceration on the bleak Bass Rock in the Firth of Forth. Henry Erskine was considered to have been the prime influence on Thomas Boston from Duns, who took charge of the church at Simprim before being inducted to Ettrick, where he spent the rest of his life. The Boston Church in Duns still records the name of the man who when in failing health preached to his Ettrick congregation propped up at his bedroom window.

The little kirk at Simprim on the Coldstream to Swinton road is now ruinous, as are many others in rural districts. Many which remain are worth a visit; Polwarth or Polart has already been mentioned in the story of Grisel Hume. Ladykirk, opposite Norham Castle, once built entirely of fireproof stone, was founded by King James IV in thanks for his narrow escape from drowning while fording the Tweed.

Fogo near Duns has a unique double 'lairds loft' where the churchyard holds poignant memories of World War II in the graves of Commonwealth airmen killed in flying accidents at nearby Charterhall. Also interred here are the remains of one 'Yorkie' or 'Border Rover' who spent much of his life wandering the Borders. Some mystery surrounds 'Yorkie' who was thought by many of the local populace to be the son of a high-ranking clergyman from that part of the world. With his collie dog at heel 'Yorkie', a truculent character held in some fear, fished the many streams throughout the Borders, where his success was often attributed to the secret potions with which his 'garden flies' were treated.

Edrom near the Duns-Chirnside road has a fine carved Norman Arch incorporated into a mausoleum dating from 1105. A relic of religion in the shape of a 10-foot high medieval 'wheel' cross can be seen near the village of Eccles, which probably marked an area of sanctuary associated with Eccles Convent.

Near Foulden Church stands one of the few surviving tithe barns to be seen in this part of the world. This harks back to the times when each farmer in the parish was duty bound to donate a tenth of his crops — a tithe — to the church. Stipends continued to be paid in kind even after tithe barns fell into disuse. In the *Statistical Account*, 1791–9 the writers, mainly parish ministers, quote their stipends in both money and kind. James Bell, DD, the minister at Coldstream, having for example £80 in money, 2 chaulders of meal and one of barley plus 12 acres of very good land. At Cranshaws, a small parish in the Lammermuirs, the total earnings for the incumbent, the Rev. George Drummond, amount to only £50 which included the

Tithe Barn at Foulden

stipend of £36 19s 5d with a glebe of 15 acres of tolerably good land.

Foulden was the scene of a meeting between representatives of James VI of Scotland and Elizabeth I of England to discuss the fate of James's mother Mary Queen of Scots. The question was, would the Scottish faction be deeply offended if the English queen ordered Mary's head to the block? Apparently not. As history records, the promise of succession by James to the English throne must have eliminated any concern for his mother.

The villages along the southern belt of the Merse along Tweedside downstream from Coldstream once rang in the early morning with the clatter of studded fishermen's boots. Ladykirk, Paxton and Hutton at one time all had salmon fishing crews working nearby fisheries. As is explained elsewhere in this book this business is now all but finished.

Many of the families renting fisheries from proprietors could trace their connection back a hundred years, as could the Fulton family with the Hotham's of Milne Graden where the Little

Littlehaugh fishery at Milne Graden (now closed)

Haugh fishery had been leased and worked by the former for five generations up until 1990.

Despite having to the south the coalfields of north Northumberland and the Lothian mining area to the north, extraction of ore and coal has never been nor is today a prominent feature in the Merse. Evidence of coal mining can be seen at Cove on the coast and the *Statistical Account of Scotland*, states that coal was once exploited at Milne Graden on Tweedside. When men dug below the soil of the Merse it was for building stone — sandstone in this instance, which is still a feature of many farms and villages throughout the district.

These quarries were dotted throughout the county and have mostly been infilled as rubbish tips by local authorities. Large quarries were located at Coldstream, Swinton and Chirnside, some of them being worked up until the present century. Only one quarrying operation still takes place at Duns where whinstone is blasted and crushed as a road-making material.

Before the re-shaping of local government in the 1970s Berwickshire boasted three burghs Eyemouth, Coldstream and Duns, a fourth Lauder being a Royal Burgh of great antiquity.

Duns, the old county town, remains the District capital which, like the other burghs of Eyemouth and Coldstream, have all lost their direct control of local affairs other than in the Community Councils.

Whae hisna' read in Border lore,
That Duns O' Ferlies hauds a' store,
Her castle, hen poo', bogs and law,
Whae disnae' ken that Duns dings a?

The present-day town of Duns occupies a site south of the original which lies below Duns Law, still known as the Bruntons ('burnt towns'). A cairn marks the site of the old town bearing the inscription:

THIS STONE MARKS THE
SITE OF THE OLD TOWN
OF DUNSE DESTROYED
IN THE BORDER RAIDS.
 1588

Duns Law was the scene in 1639 of the encampment by General Alexander Leslie's Covenanting army awaiting conflict with the forces of King Charles I.

Despite the threat, battle never ensued; Charles thought better of trying to impose Episcopalism upon Scotland. More especially when these Covenanters who, on planting their standard on Duns Law had taken an oath, 'For Christ's Crown and Covenant', meaning they would fight to the death.

A cavalcade to Duns Law led by the Riever and his Lass is the main outing during the Duns festival week which features a service and an oration by a guest speaker. Still to be seen on Duns Law are the earthworks of Leslie's camp and the stone where his standard was raised. Like Hume Crag, Duns Law makes an excellent viewpoint of the Merse looking out over the roofs of Duns below.

Born in 1266 at Duns was the most famous scholar, theologian and philosopher of the time, John Dunse Scotus. It may appear strange that Scotus's name is remembered as dunce — a poor scholar at book learning. This came about, we are told, in the Commonwealth period when strict Puritans sought to deride the theories and teachings of John Dunse Scotus. On the seven hundredth anniversary of his birth in 1966 two bronze monuments were erected by the Franciscan Order of the Catholic Church to commemorate the event. One is situated in Duns public park, whilst the other, marking the birthplace of Scotus, stands at the lodges leading to Duns Castle, beside the entrance to the Duns Castle Nature Reserve.

The Duns park memorial takes the shape of a statue, while that at Duns castle in the form of a plaque is more informative:

> John Duns Scotus
> The Subtle Doctor
> And Member of the Franciscan Order
> Was born on this site in 1266
> Wherever his distinguished name is uttered
> He sheds lustre on Duns and Scotland
> The Town and Land what bore him

In 1991 Scotus was declared 'Venerable' by the Pope, perhaps the first step to sainthood championed by the archdiocese of Cologne in Germany, the Diocese of Nola in Italy and the Franciscan Order. From seven hundred years ago the memory of Scotus still remains strong on the Continent although his name and work based on the theology of Mary and the Immaculate Conception is virtually unknown in his native land.

Covering a total of 32 hectares the Duns Castle Nature Reserve was the first such site to be organised by the Scottish Wildlife Trust. Established in the 1970s the Reserve was the brainchild of the late Lieutenant-Colonel G. H. Hay and local ornithologist Alec Cowieson. Eight Hectares of the reserve are taken up by the Hen Poo — heron pond — an artificial lake which could be considered the main focus. Naturally waterfowl are a feature of the Hen Poo but within the mixed woodland 62 bird species have been recorded. These find a home among the 32 tree species, 10 different shrubs set among a variety of 34 wild flower and shared by 11 mammals.

Several houses in the Merse bear the title of 'castle'. Duns, however, is the only one which can claim to date from the days when this meant a defensive building. Duns Castle is built around a Pele Tower dating from 1320 given to the Earl of Moray by King Robert the Bruce. In 1696 The Earl of Tweedale purchased Duns Castle for his son, William Hay of

Duns Scotus, Duns Public Park

Drummelzier, where since this time the Hay family have been in unbroken occupation.

Between 1818 and 1822 the architect, James Gillespie Graham, undertook the enlargement and embellishment of the building into its present Gothic Revival form. Alexander

Judging Sheep Duns Show

Hay, the present owner, is dedicated to retaining the character of Duns Castle; any internal alterations are for modern comfort and conservation purposes. While Duns Castle is not normally open to the public it is available to private and business guests for meetings, overnight stays, lunches and dinners.

Duns Show, or rather the Berwickshire County Show, organised by the Berwickshire Agricultural Association, is held annually in the grounds of Duns Castle. Inevitably as a one-day event it is a smaller affair than the Border Union Show but represents just the same a cross-section of farming and country life.

Attendance figures are very much dependent upon the vagaries of the weather as the date now clashes with the harvesting of winter-sown grain crops. Organisers and machinery dealers are unsure whether to hope for wet weather to curtail harvesting for the day and bring the farmers or for dry weather to bring the casual visitor.

Here the pride of Berwickshire's cattle herds and sheep flocks are on display in competition with their peers for championship awards. In the three rings can be found horse-jumping for children and adults, a parade of livestock, and in the main ring some feature of entertainment which will appeal to non-agriculturalists. Local organisations and charities take the opportunity to set out their stall at Duns Show in either a fund-raising or public relations exercise or a combination of both.

At Newtown Street in Duns, the Jim Clark Trophy Collection is on view, dedicated to the twice world champion racing car driver in 1963 and 1965 who was killed in Germany in 1968. Jim farmed nearby at Edington near the village of Chirnside, but he became the first Honorary Burgess of Duns in 1965, a year after receiving an OBE from the Queen in recognition of his contribution to motor sport. Honours were heaped upon the Borders driver who was not only a competitor on the Grand Prix scene but also drove in rallies and speed trials and was the first British winner of the American Indianapolis 500. What is on display is a small part of the trophies won by Jim Clark and presented to Duns by Jim's parents. The collection is administered by trustees of the Jim Clark Memorial Room which has received over 200,000 visitors since opening twenty years ago.

Driving exclusively for Lotus in Grand Prix events the unassuming Berwickshire farmer not only possesed superb driving skills, he was also at one with his cars, as in the 1965 race at Silverstone when he nursed a badly misfiring engine home three seconds ahead of Graham Hill. Jim Clark was without doubt one of, the greatest if not the greatest Grand Prix driver of his time. In 1963 he was the youngest driver of all time to achieve the championship. Seven Grand Prix wins fell to Jim in one year — a record for the time when there were fewer races in this event than there are today. It was a sad moment when the workers from Edington carried Jim Clark's body the last few paces into Chirnside churchyard. Jim Clark was known as, and is remembered in Berwickshire not only as a world champion, but as one of nature's gentlemen who remained untouched by worldwide fame. A memorial clock raised by local subscription stands at Crosshill in Chirnside, while even more than twenty years after his death a steady stream of visitors continues to visit

Jim Clark (D. Smith Photo Centre)

the Duns Trophy Room and Clark's last resting place in Chirnside.

Agriculture and fast driving seem to make easy companions for Berwickshire farmers, since Louise Aitken-Walker, who hails originally from Langton Mill near Duns, is the current Ladies World Champion rally driver. Rallying began for Louise when her brothers entered her in the Ford sponsored, 'Find a Lady Rally Driving Champion' in 1979. Since then Louise has became a leading exponent in the art of making saloon cars cover a remarkable distance over unsuitable roads in a ridiculously short time. Her achievements include winning the Group 1 National Open Rally Championship, and the Group A 1600 British Open Championship. In 1989 came the Ladies European Championship and in 1990 Louise won the World Ladies Championship at the wheel of a Vauxhall Astra. The sponsorship wheel has come full circle. For the 1991–2 season Louise is to drive for Ford who were the instigators of her career back in 1979. No doubt we will be seeing more of this Berwickshire lass over the coming years speeding through special stages in a shower of mud and grit.

In Duns's fine public park a short walk from the Market Square a further monument to John Dunse Scotus can be found along with the war memorial to both world wars. Also found here is the town's old market cross which once stood on the site of the old town hall within the market square. Within the same arc near the entrance gates stands another granite memorial, the Duns Polish War Memorial, bearing the inscription:

> Remembering the 127 Polish Soldiers of the First and Second Armoured Regiment Stationed at Duns 1941–1944 and Fallen on the Battlefields of France Belgium Holland and Germany.

Manderston, considered to be the finest example of an Edwardian mansion anywhere in Britain, is situated a mile or so east of Duns near the A6105 Duns to Berwick road. The home of Lord and Lady Palmer, Manderston is said to be the swansong of the great classical house. This is not surprising as within the house there are magnificent state rooms and the only staircase in the world with a silver balustrade. As seen today Manderston and its grounds are the result of enhancements carried out mainly by Sir James Miller, whose father Sir William had been involved in exporting herring to Russia. It is said that Sir James embarked upon a scheme of improvements to impress his wife's aristocartic relations. Whether he succeeded or not is unknown, but the heritage is a superb example of turn-of-the-century craftsmanship in all building mediums. The splendour extends to the formal gardens where every gate is adorned with statues. Bronze and marble fountains play amid the beds which must have required an army of gardeners to keep them in order. A mock tower near the gardens has on the ground floor a marble dairy lined with marble from seven countries, cool even on the hottest summer day. The traditional implements of butter-making line the smooth icy workbenches. Above, in a room beautifully pannelled in Spanish oak, Lady Miller and her friends took tea provided by the dairymaid living nearby who had her own discreet staircase to serve the guests.

Manderston stables must be the best example of equine accommodation anywhere, with the stalls of hardwood bearing the names of their occupants in brass and marble. Within the harness room even the workbench is of exquisite marble and the floor is set in a pattern of black and white marble tiles.

Manderston grounds are laid out around an artificial lake where woodland walks can be enjoyed by visitors among shrubs and mature trees. Indoors Lord Palmer has on display his own unique collection of Huntley and Palmer's decorative biscuit tins, his lordship being a member of this internationally famous firm of bakers.

Crumstane Farm Park lies nearby, on the road between Duns and Chirnside. Opened in 1990 the park is part of a working farm, but with a difference. Here farmer Joe Burn has established a collection of over sixty different species of livestock and poultry, many of these once common on farms throughout the Merse but now replaced by breeds which give a better commercial return. Highland, Longhorn and Dexter cattle, rare sheep breeds such as Southdown and Hebridean, goats, pigs, including the wrinkle-faced Vietnamese pot-bellied pig are but some. Crumstane Farm Park is a regular outing for many schools in the Borders. Even children living on farms today where few livestock are raised have the opportunity to encounter many breeds of farm stock at close quarters. Star of

Children from Chirnside school make friends with Prince at Crumstane Farm Park

Crumstane without doubt is Prince the Clydesdale, whose predecessors were once the prime movers for the cultivation and harvest of the Merse. A gentle giant, Prince knows the rustle of a bag of feed nuts. Under the supervision of Joe Burn even the youngest visitor can give Prince a treat.

Due north from Manderstone a simple stone monument marks the last resting place of a French knight, Anthony D'Arcy or Seigneur de la Bastie. D'Arcy had arrived in Scotland to compete in the grand tournaments organised at the court of James IV, having toured Europe at such events challenging all comers to mortal combat. Regent Albany had appointed D'Arcy Warden of the Eastern Marches instead of Alexander, the 3rd Lord Home, whose family had traditionally held the post. D'Arcy then was not a popular figure in the Merse where he was already suspect as being party to the later execution of Lord Home and his brother. Simmering resentment grew to open conflict when D'Arcy encountered a party under David Home of Wedderburn near Langton west of Duns. Despite the Home's part being smaller than that of the warden the latter

fled for the safety of Dunbar Castle. Towards Duns with the
Home's in hot pursuit, crossing the Pouterlany Burn at a place
called Corney Ford:

> As Bawtie fled frae Langton Tower,
> Wi his troops along the way,
> By the Corney-Foord ane auld man stood,
> And to him did Bawtie say
>
> Pri'thee tell unto me thou weird auld man,
> Whilk name this ford doth bear,
> Tis the Corney-Foord, quoth the weird auld man,
> And thoult cross it alive nae mair.

Through the town of Duns and on towards Broomhouse
Tower where D'Arcy's horse foundered in a bog. Some versions
of the story give David Home credit for slaying D'Arcy;
others say it was a page. Whichever is correct the handsome
Frenchman was buried where he lay, his head borne off as
a grisly trophy to moulder on the battlements of Hume or
Wedderburn Castle. A Home of nearby Broomhouse raised the
monument the following year with local placenames of Bawties
or Basties field remembering the event:

> And they've set his head on the towering' wa
> O' the castle o' Hume sae high,
> To moulder there i' the sun and wind
> Till mony long years gae bye!
>
> The Leddies o' France may wail and mourn,
> May wail and mourn fu' sair,
> For the bonny Bawties long brown locks,
> They'll ner see waving mair!

Travelling south to the Border Coldstream claims to be the 'first
true Border toon', whose motto *Nuli secondus* translates from
Latin as 'second to none', England being but a mere stone's
throw across Tweed:

> We shall always lead,
> On the silvery Tweed,
> We're the first true Border toon,
> We can proudly say this is Coldstream's day,
> We're a jewel in Scotia's croon.

Coldstream is better known than any other small comparable Border town because of giving its name to the 2nd Regiment of Foot of the British Army, only the Grenadier Guards taking precedence of the Coldstreams. Founded by General Monck, the regiment was raised at Berwick on Tweed in 1650 from part of the Fenwick's and Hesilrige's regiments whose campaign in the south of Scotland included the Battle of Dunbar on 3 September 1650.

Following Cromwell's death in 1658 Monck was instrumental in assisting to restore the Monarchy in 1660, throwing his support to the Royalist faction. Some accounts say that Monck's men laid down their arms for the Commonwealth and picked them up for Charles II at Coldstream; other historians say that this symbolic gesture took place at Tower Hill. By the end of 1659 Monck had established his headquarters at Coldstream before setting off south where the regiment's first task was to quell civil disorder. Their march to London began on 1 January 1660, taking thirty-four days, the soldiers arriving in the caital with their feet bound with rags and sacking, their boots destroyed in the arduous march. It was only after the death of Monck that the regiment assumed the name of the Coldstream Guards. It has the distinction of being not only the oldest corps by continuous existence in the British Army, but also the sole representative by direct descent of the first regular army raised by Oliver Cromwell.

Strong links remain between the regiment and the town whose name it bears. The freedom of the burgh was granted to them in 1968, while a small contingent always attends the annual Civic Week celebrations. Also the prize list for the local school is provided each year by The Guards. Coldstream Museum in the market square on the site of a house said to have been general Monk's headquarters, displays items donated by the regiment and a glimpse of the past history of the town.

Not that The Guards were the first military visitors. Standing at a suitable fording place Coldstream must have seen many an army cross back and forth over the Tweed here. The town's local name *Castrum* has Roman connections, being translated from the Latin as 'cold stream'. A Roman camp exists at Belchester near Leitholm, while a signal station was sited on

Nuns Walks Coldstream, Charlies Monument & Smeatons Bridge
plaque shows level of 1948 flood

a prominent knoll alongside The Mount — a motte near the
farm of Castlelaw.

Where the Leet Water meets Tweed a convent once stood
overlooking the Tweed Green where the ford is thought to have
been located prior to the construction of John Smeaton's bridge
built in the 1760s. Founded by Gospatrick, Earl of Dunbar,
around 1165 nothing now remains of the convent other than
a burial vault.

A nunnery attached to Coldstream was established at the
village of Eccles to the north and a cross at Crosshall farm
may have marked the bounds of sanctuary around this
establishment. Further grounds and a church were given
at The Hirsel together with lands in the medieval town of
Derchester (Darnchester) of which no trace remains. Edward
I visited Coldstream in 1290, returning again in March 1296
with 500 horse and 30,000 infantry, who seemed to have
caused extensive damage in their billeting, although there is
no evidence of actual deliberate destruction.

Tradition has it that the Prioress from Coldstream arranged

for the nobility among the slain at Flodden to be brought back to Coldstream for burial either here on Tweed Green or at the Hirsel. On the level ground between Tweed and Leet Water Coldstream's market place indicates that once when the river had to be crossed by ford this and not the High Street was the principal trading area of the town.

Flodden Field over the Border, which is near the village of Branxton and not Flodden Hill, is the main rideout of the Coldstream Civic Week during the first week of August. Led by the Coldstreamer, a young man elected or nominated to carry the town flag for the week, the cavalcade crosses into Northumbria to pay homage to the, 'Dead of both Nations' as the simple inscription on the granite cross erected by the Berwickshire Naturalist Society relates.

Flodden was a black day in Scottish history and for many years afterwards the Borderland was much weakened and open to attack. Historians may still argue as to the reason why the Scots suffered such a crushing defeat when they were the larger army in a stronger position. Two versions of the death of King James exist, the most common being that in a desperate last stand around the king there fell the cream of the Scottish nobility and churchmen.

Another version has him engaged in the first impetuous charge downhill from Branxton Hill which foundered in the boggy ground at the base. Here the shorter English bill proved superior to the long spears of the Scots, the hacking edge slashing the spears' shafts, leaving the Scots defenceless. On drawing their swords to engage at close quarters they were now out-reached by the bills to be cut down where they stood.

It was as much the superiority of the bill as the skill of the English archers which as led to the fatal rout. One cannot help wondering what fate befell the dependents of the ordinary fighting man, 'the flower of the forest'. Did they and their children experience destitution, poverty and hunger following the adventure of king James?

Overlooking Coldstream from his lofty perch at the east end is Charlie's Monument, raised in honour of Charles Marjoribanks of the nearby Lees after his election as first M. P. for Berwickshire following the introduction of the Reform Bill in 1832.

Coldstream can boast one of the best views of the Tweed from Henderson Park, almost in the town centre, downstream to Coldstream Bridge and south towards the Cheviots sometimes blue and distant, sometimes in different atmospheric conditions seeming near enough to touch.

A granite plinth records the occasion when the Guards received the freedom of the burgh in August 1968. It fails to mention the sorry heids induced by the hospitality provided at the Guards' camp on the school playing fields. Also holding the freedom is our own Border regiment, the Kings Own Scottish Borderers, Lord Home and the late Hans Lanmack. Hans served on the burgh council for many years — several as provost — and was instrumental in enhancing the relationship between the regiment and town.

Smeaton's bridge must have been a wonder of its time. No longer was the transport of goods north and south dependent upon whether or not Tweed was in spate. Commerce could take place now come flood or high water. The toll house attached to the Coldstream Bridge, perhaps also once an inn, had in its time a reputation for runaway marriages. Indeed Coldstream must have been a handy place for elopements, as no fewer than three Lord Chancellors of England, Lords Eldon, Erskine and Brougham took the opportunity of tying the marital knot here at the first available place once off English soil.

In the middle of last century William Dickson seemed to have conducted the marriage business in a proper manner, keeping a register of couples wed in circumstances which were then entirely legal. Apparently the local minister, Thomas Smith Goldie, took exception to this and commenced proceedings in Edinburgh. But Dickson won the case and was carried shoulder high through the town.

On the occasion when Robert Burns ventured into England in May 1787 it was by Coldstream Bridge, over the central arch the Coldstream Burns Club, the second oldest in Scotland recorded in bronze his words on that occasion:

> O Scotia my dear my native soil,
> To whom my warmest wish is sent,
> Long may thy hardy sons of rustic toil,

Be blessed with peace and sweet content.

The Coldstream Country trail continues downstream from the Bridge by the riverside to first, the village of Lennel, then to the old churchyard which marks the site of the original Lennel village. The trail makes a pleasant outing to Lennel churchyard where Scott set Marmion in the church ruins on the eve of Flodden.

'Stung with these thoughts, he urged to speed
His troop, and reached, at eve, the Tweed,
Where Lenell's convent closed their march;
(there now is left but one frail arch,'

From Coldstream it is but a mile to The Hirsel, home of the Douglas Home family, the descendants of the March Wardens of long ago. The Homes appear to have arrived at the Hirsel on a permanent basis early in the seventeenth century, when, in 1611, the first Earl exchanged £40,000 Scots, the lands of Jedburgh and theirs in Roxburghshire, Lanarkshire, Dumfriesshire and Stirlingshire for the lands of Hirsel with Sir John Kerr of Hirsel, and adopted the subsidiary title of Lord Coldingham instead of Lord Jedburgh.

The present Lord Home disclaimed his titles for life in order to re-enter The House of Commons following the death of his father in 1951. Lord Home is best known as having held the post of Prime Minister in the conservative Government from 1963–4 which was the culmination of a lifetime devoted to political life.

What is unique about the Hirsel, (the name signifies the amount of land which could be tended by a single shepherd), is that the grounds have been continually open to the public for many years. Originally a permit system was in operation but later this developed to free access to all. A small charge is made today for the upkeep of paths and the other facilities. Of all the woodland walks around the Hirsel the best known is Dundock, a wood blown down in the same storm which caused the East Coast Fishing Disaster in October 1881. At the time this was replanted with rhododendrons and azaleas, the peat used to create the ideal conditions for these shrubs being transported

Hirsel Homestead Museum and Visitor Centre

20 miles by horse-drawn cart, from Bunkle beyond Duns, which then formed part of the Douglas Home estates.

A lake was formed from a boggy part of land at the same time, and today this forms a sanctuary for duck, geese and other wet land bird species. In recent years the old Homestead at the Hirsel has been converted into a museum and visitor centre depicting rural crafts of past years. A room is dedicated to the archaeological finds made around the Hirsel. Artifacts date back to stone age times but the emphasis is upon a major 'dig' which unearthed a medieval church and cemetery.

Craft fairs are held at least once a year at and around the visitor centre, while for over a decade the sheltered aspect of the Hirsel proved an ideal situation for the Borders County Fair, a popular two-day charity event now discontinued. Not that Hirsel visitor centre is entirely centred on the past; several craftsmen and women are now established workers in wood, clay, semi-precious stones, wool and leather.

Homes or Humes have already been mentioned as branches of the family-held lands almost everywhere across The Merse.

These included the castles of Ayton and Wedderburn, today still shown as castles but in reality fairly 'modern' buildings. Ayton, now owned by the Liddel-Grainger family was designed by James Gillespie Graham, whose work also includes Brodick Castle on the Isle of Arran, for William Mitchell-Innes, Governor of the Bank of Scotland in the mid-nineteenth century. Without a doubt the builders chose wisely in selecting the site as Ayton Castle somehow manages to have a commanding view over the Eye Valley while managing to find shelter from the cold winds of winter from the North Sea. Ayton Castle continues to be a family home but is open to the public on Sundays during the summer months. Corporate entertainment in the form of clay-pigeon shooting and cross-country driving, with professional tuition if required, is available in the grounds of Ayton Castle. Instruction in polo, a new sport for the Borders, is also offered.

At Wedderburn Castle, the seat of David Home already mentioned in this chapter, the present building may be the fourth to occupy the site. A plaque in the courtyard is said to belong to one of the earlier buildings. Wedderburn was built for Patrick Home by Robert Adam and was possibly the first Georgian Mansion to be built in this style.

Wedderburn remains as the builders left it; in fact until coming into the present ownership internal painting had only taken place twice during the past two hundred years. Currently the present owners use Wedderburn as a display area for antique furniture where visitors are welcome to browse. Other plans include the development of a restaurant once the building is restored to its former Georgian glory, including repainting in the original Adam colours.

As has been already related, the family of Home played a major role in the making of the Eastern March. Like many other families of nobility in the Borders and beyond the known history of the Home's is traceable to post-Norman times.

One Berwickshire family, the Swintons, can go even further back into pre-Norman times. From Edulf, 1st Lord of Bamburgh, who ruled over Bernicia in the late 9th century, the Swinton family can trace an unbroken lineage to the present day. By 1098 the lands of Swinton were granted to Liulf de Swynton by King Edgar when the family moved north of the

Tweed to escape William the Conqueror's, 'Harrying of the North.' Documents held in Durham confirming the grant of Swinton to Ernulf de Swinton in 1140 are among the earliest records of Scottish inheritance.

Through the centuries several branches of the family became established in the Merse, including Swinton of Swinton, Swinton of that Ilk and Swinton of Kimmerghame. Throughout this time the Saxon forename Edulf was used up until this century, most recently by the late Reverend Alan Edulf Swinton, the last Swinton of Swinton, for many years a well loved Priest-in-Charge of St Mary's and All Souls at Coldstream.

Set into the south wall of Swinton Kirk is a sandstone effigy of a recumbent figure surmounted by a chained boar and three piglets, dedicated to Alan Swinton, the 7th baron. Legend has it that the Swintons gained their land and title through this Sir Alan de Swinton slaying a wild boar which had previously terrorised the countryside.

In the 1791–2 Statistical Account the Rev. George Cupples gives this story as 'gospel', even citing the location where the deed took place as a field at Swintonhill known as Alan's Cairn. This story is nowhere recorded in the long documentation of the Swinton family, and, logical as it may appear, seems to be merely a mythical piece of folklore.

Sir Walter Scott wrongly connects Sir Alan de Swinton, who died sometime after 1247, with the battle of Halidon Hill near Berwick. He, like the Turnbull who did figure in this battle, was a man of giant stature. An extraordinary large human skull found in the vaults below Swinton Kirk is said to be Sir Alan's, a cast of which was made and presented to Sir Walter.

It was at Homildon Hill near Wooler that another Swinton, Sir John, who had played a prominent part in the Battle of Otterburn in 1388, led his small band of Scots in a desperate charge against a larger English force. Even while knowing that death was inevitable he urged his men forward, 'rather than stand and be slaughtered like deer by the enemy archers'.

Traditionally the Swintons have been soldiers both at home and abroad, and as can be seen above were never far away from Border conflicts. Some idea of the troubled times which existed in the Eastern March can be gauged from the fact that in 1402

Border Counties Fair, The Hirsel catapult range

Sir John Swinton, 11th of that Ilk, obtained land and the Tower of Cranshaws in the Lammermuirs in order to be more remote from the turmoil nearer the Border.

Up until the Civil War this branch of the family held Cranshaws, when John Swinton, 20th of that Ilk, was a supporter of Oliver Cromwell, while his brothers were Royalists. Upon the Restoration all the lands of Swinton, including Cranshaws, were forfeited and given to the Duke of Lauderdale. A long and expensive legal battle to lift the forfeiture ensued, which the Swintons finally won in 1690. The costs incurred, however, meant that the lands at Cranshaws had to be sold.

Swinton Kirk was rebuilt in 1729, but dates from around 1100. In addition to Sir Alan's tomb, which must date from the earlier building, below the gallery there is also retained an aumbry used to store elements and sacred vessels for saying mass in Catholic times. All around the kirk are memorials to Swintons down through the years, while the chained boar

Swinton crest appears in finely carved wooden figures either side of the Communion Table.

Among the memorials is one to Campbell Swinton who developed in theory the principle of modern television. While the construction of the first working television is rightly attributed to John Logie Baird's mechanical set, Campbell Swinton's concept was based upon the familiar cathode-ray tube electronic machine familiar today in every home in the land.

In Berwickshire today the Kimmerghame branch of the Swinton family is represented by Major-General Sir John Swinton who, as Lord Lieutenant of the county, is HM Queen Elizabeth's representative in the Merse. Sir John's duties in this office must be of a more pleasurable nature than the equivalent post of long ago, that of Warden of the Eastern March of Scotland held by his ancestor, also John Swinton 18th of that Ilk in the 16th century.

On the porch of Swinton Kirk can be found a sundail erected as a memorial to the local farming family of Brewis. The inscription thereon is an appropriate one on which to leave The Merse:

'While the earth remaineth, seedtime and harvest shall not cease.'

# CHAPTER 4

## *Berwick on Tweed — The Scottish Connection*

Few of the old Scottish shires could boast, or should it be, lament, that the town from which that county was named retained neither administrative nor political links with that county, having in fact for the past five centuries been situated in a different country. This unique case prevailed between Berwickshire, otherwise, the County of Berwick and The Borough of Berwick on Tweed, a frontier town which suffered mightily at the hands of both Scots and English.

Berwick Borough today covers an area far beyond the old town bounds, but is an English town administering jointly with the Northumbria County Council this north-east corner of England: a curious state of affairs for one of Scotland's earliest Royal Burghs which was in former times the country's principal seaport. Berwick nevertheless retains strong links with both Berwickshire, the Borders and Scotland.

This anomaly can best be explained by having a look at Berwick's history. Its early origins are veiled by time but most likely the name is an adaptation of 'bar wyk' — the barley town. Some sources cite the coat of arms, a bear chained below a tree, as a reflection of this name, 'bear and wych' (wych elm). With the Border established at the river Tweed in 1018 Berwick for the first time became part of Scotland, whereafter it is mentioned as a Scottish Royal Burgh in 1120. Berwick increased in importance throughout the twelfth century becoming during this period the principal port for Scotland and having revenues exceeding those of Leith and Aberdeen. After sacking Berwick in 1296, Edward I saw the potential of the town as a military base for his lifelong mission to be the hammer of the Scots, Robert Bruce recaptured it in 1318 but after the disaster for the Scots at Halidon Hill just outside the town in 1333 Berwick returned to English control.

This was but one occasion, taken overall from 1173 up to the time when the Scots finally gave up the struggle in 1482.

Ownership changed by battle or treaty on no less than thirteen occasions.

Trade appears to have dwindled after the town's destruction by Edward I in 1296. Even so, in 1330, the year after the death of Robert Bruce, Berwick's harbour dues standing at £549 were the highest in Scotland. During the same year Edinburgh could only muster £400, Aberdeen £484, with Perth and Dundee straggling at £88 and £85 respectively. The *Lanercost Chronicle* describes Berwick as being, 'a second Alexandria, whose riches was the sea and water around its walls', custom dues to the value of £2,190 being collected in 1286.

Berwick's importance, both commercially and strategically in medieval times was such that it was known as the 'Key to the Border', with the majority of Scottish abbeys holding property in the town. Even after 1482 the threat of recapture by the Scots remained real, and was only removed with the ascension of James VI of Scotland to the English throne. Berwick seems then to have been regarded more as an outpost on foreign soil, a Kyber Pass fort rather than part of England proper.

The Berwick garrison were well pleased with the new situation greeting James's arrival en route south to assume the new role with a salute of musket and gunfire. It was King James who, in 1604, endorsed the present Border three miles north of the Tweed at Lamberton, creating Berwick as something of a separate entity outwith either Scotland or England.

Berwick Bounds were set to include not only the town, but also what is known as 'The Liberty of Berwick' a triangular tract of land reaching over three miles upstream along Tweed's banks, running north for two, then north-east for a further two miles to Lamberton, then following the coastline south-east back to Berwick.

A symbolic ceremony of Riding the Bounds takes place on 1st May every year, confirming the Borough boundaries, where many of the farms are the property of the freemen of Berwick. Unlike the Scottish Border burghs who conduct Common Ridings for the same purpose, Berwick has no election of principles and the event only occupies half a day.

A separate identity for the town continued into the nineteenth century, Berwick receiving mention in Acts of Parliament akin to another country within the Union. Parliamentary Acts refer to 'Scotland, England and Berwick on Tweed'. For some reason a peace treaty with Russia failed to mention Berwick and until recently the town could claim it was still at war with the inheritors of the Tzars.

That then was the one-time extent of Berwick. The present-day Borough of Berwick on Tweed encompasses a large tract of north Northumbria stretching south to Wooler and Glendale and west along Tweedside to the Roxburgh District boundary. Prior to the mid-1970s changes in local government the Borough comprised Berwick on the north bank and Tweedmouth and Spittal on the south, these two towns having been purchased in 1657 by the Corporation of Berwick from the Earl of Suffolk, but not included in the Borough until 1835.

Even today most native 'Twempies' from Tweedmouth or 'Spittalers', would feel mildly insulted if referred to as Berwickers, an attitude shared by those who belong to Berwick considering themselves Berwickers before Northumbrian or English.

Spittal was a one-time spa town attracting many visitors during the late nineteenth-century boom for taking the waters and sea bathing. Spittal denotes a hospital — in this case that of St Bartholomew, established sometime in the early thirteenth century for the care of lepers.

Mentioning Spittal to longer-in-the-tooth Borderers means one thing — Spittal Trip, the annual seaside Sunday School outing of the past by train and now by bus. Spittal Trip was, until the 1960s, when car ownership became general, often the only opportunity for children from inland towns to visit the eternal mecca of the young, the seaside. Even today, when holidaymakers are as aquainted with the beaches of the Med as those of home, many Borderers can still recall the anticipation before the pleasure of the annual outing to Spittal. The Spittal ferry plying back and forth to Berwick Quay, taking trippers surfeit on meat pie, sticky buns and fizzy lemonade, which were the standard hand-out on Spittal Trips, across the river to the delights of 'Woolies' in Marygate.

Certain local worthies could always be found on these Sunday school outings, their arrival at Spittal usually coinciding with a raging thirst brought on by the journey. Emerging with thirst quenched from a Spittal hostelry, the head worthy of one

Marygate on market day, Scotsgate in background

Tweedside town encountered a weeping child, still clutching his brown paper bag, containing meat pie, sticky bun and fizzy lemonade. Despite being something of a rough diamond our worthy was a humane soul, and so he enquired of the wailing infant as to the reason for this distress. Between sobs the child managed to blurt out, 'A've lost ma mam'. 'Lost yir mam' replied the worthy, 'this is Spittal Trip bairn, never mind yer mither; eat yer pie'. A phrase of the moment which caught on for decades, long after that worthy was beneath the sod, too gripe or moan about any matter in his home town would draw the response: 'awe never mind yer mither; eat yer pie.'

Having such a turbulent history it is natural that fortifications and Berwick on Tweed go hand in hand. During the height of these violent wrangles employment for masons and builders must certainly have been assured, as fire and onslaught destroyed the fabric of the town.

In the Elizabethan Walls Berwick on Tweed can claim the best surviving example of town fortifications anywhere in Europe, enclosing part of the old town. The design of the town walls follows principles attributed to the Italian engineers, Contio and Portinari, being laid out in such a manner that no matter where besiegers pressed upon the defences they could be subject to withering cross-fire from one or other of the protruding bastions.

The work was at least partially completed by 1565, as by this time they were said to have been in a defensive state. Elaborate precautions, which never saw a shot fired in anger, were declared finally redundant when James VI of Scotland passed through the town on his way south to assume the English Crown.

Their original purpose as a defence against the Scots was never put to the test, but it must be noted that in both 1715 and 1745 the Jacobites gave the town a wide berth. Later wars saw Berwick heavily garrisoned and the walls defended. During the Napoleonic Wars 54 cannon were installed along the ramparts with a kenspeckle array of troops ranging from three Independent Companies of Invalids to the Gentlemen's Independent Volunteers.

Visitors to Berwick should not miss a walk around The Walls; the going is quite easy and the circuit can be completed by those in a hurry in around three-quarters of an hour. Guided tours are given in the summer months starting at the Barracks, so here, at what is known as 'The Parade', where car parking is available, is an apt place to make a start.

Defences around Berwick had been subject to repeated updating from medieval times, those built in 1565 being the successors of a much earlier wall and ditch system, itself improved and strengthened by Edward I. This arrangements, while lacking the sophistication of the Elizabethan Walls, withstood sieges over a month long.

Part of these older works, and therefore part of the town, fell outside the Elizabethan structure and can be seen most easily near the holiday camp and golf course. In the lower part of the town, in particular along the riverside, the new walls more or less followed the line taken by the earlier fortifications, being built upon and upgraded to meet the new specification. The prominent octagonal Bell Tower standing on a medieval base was primarily a watch tower to give warning of the approach of danger from land or sea.

Old Bridge Berwick on Tweed


King James, on leaving Berwick on his journey to London was far from enthralled by the rickety wooden structure which then served as a bridge over the Tweed. Some accounts say that he only crossed in dire fear of his life, so it is not surprising that one of his first acts as ruler of the united kingdoms was to order the building of a new bridge at Berwick.

Work commenced in 1611, but it was not until 23 years later that what is known as the Old Bridge, the James VI Bridge, or 'Auld Brig' to those who use it frequently, was finally completed. A short distance upstream the wooden piles or foundations of the older structure can still be seen at low tide. A piece of local folklore has it that firm foundations for the Auld Brig were so difficult to obtain that at least some of the piers supporting the fifteen red sandstone arches were founded upon large packs of wool.

Up until 1928 the Old Bridge carried the main Great North Road over the Tweed estuary and through the narrow streets of Berwick. Its replacement, the Royal Tweed Bridge, was opened in that year by HRH the Prince of Wales, later the Duke of Windsor. Comprising four reinforced concrete arches, that on the northernmost bank at 361 feet being cited as one of the longest such structures in the country, the Royal Tweed Bridge is invariably referred to as simply the New Brig or Bridge.

Construction of the New Bridge which brought traffic through Tweedmouth then into Berwick at Golden Square, apparently gave its builders the same difficulties as their predecessors encountered in 1611. A total of 186 two-ton 36-foot long concrete piles were inserted to obtain a firm base in the river bed.

In turn the New Bridge has been replaced by a modern bridge a mile upstream on the Berwick bypass opened in the 1980s. Prior to the introduction of the bypass Berwick's town centre all but ground to a halt during peak periods, as most commercial traffic could only pass single file through the narrow Scotsgate above Marygate.

Upstream from Berwick's New Bridge carrying the main east coast rail route the Royal Border Bridge stands as a monument to Victorian engineering. Measuring 2,160 feet in length, 126 feet at its highest point and carried by 28 stone arches, its design was by Robert Stephenson, son of George, the pioneer of steam locomotion.

Queen Victoria opened the Royal Border (hence the 'Royal' in its title) on 29 August 1850, when, despite many elaborate preparations for the event, the royal train tarried for a brief ten minutes. As the Tweed had not marked the Border for some 400 years at the time it was perhaps some fancy of Victorian romanticism which introduced Border to its name.

Adolf Hitler was one who appreciated the strategic importance of the Royal Border Bridge in the battle being waged against his forces. Several bombing raids were launched against the RBB without result, other than unfortunately a number of civilian casualties. Berwick on Tweed is the only station available to rail travellers within the Borders region, while the recent electrification of the east coast line remains an important link in the communications network for both the Borders and north Northumbria. A recently introduced bus service rail link serving the Borders is timed to suit rail schedules.

A short distance upstream from the Royal Border Bridge are the stairs known as the 'Breakynecks' (have a look and you will immediately realize why!), descend from the site of the Berwick Castle by the White Wall of late thirteenth-century vintage to the Water Tower. Above the White Wall overlooking the Tweed estuary can be seen the Constable Tower, the most intact remainder of Berwick castle.

As to the rest, nineteenth-century railway engineers completed the work of centuries of assault, weathering and casual quarrying upon the stronghold. It was a simple matter of enough explosives in the right place to clear a site for Berwick railway station whose platforms now occupy the site of the castle's great hall.

It was here on 17 November 1292 that Edward I, Hammer of the Scots, before the full Parliament of England and much of the Scottish nobility, denied Robert Bruce's claim to the Scottish throne in favour of John Baliol. Later Edward had the Countess of Buchan imprisoned in an iron cage on the battlements for daring to have placed the Scottish crown on Bruce's head at Scone.

After his execution part of Wallace's body was displayed in the town as a deterrent to others who sought to challenge the might of Edward. Wallace is still remembered in Berwick today in the place-name of Wallace Green.

Opposite the church across The Parade, reputed incidently to have its own ghost, stand Berwick Barracks, completed in 1721 as one of the first purpose-built Barrack blocks in Britain. Here again Berwick's Scottish link is encountered, an English town having from 1888 until 1964 a garrison of the Kings Own Scottish Borderers, a Scottish regiment which is now to be amalgamated with the Royal Scots.

The regiment was founded in Edinburgh in 1689 by David Leslie, Earl of Leven, who, in the space of two hours, raised a regiment of foot for the defence of the city. To commemorate this act and also the gallant behaviour of the regiment at the Battle of Killicrankie, Edinburgh city magistrates conferred upon Leven's regiment the unique right of recruiting by beat of drum in the city, and the right to march through the city at any time with colours flying, drums beating, and bayonets fixed.

Today the old barracks host the museum of the KOSB regiment or 'Kosbies', as they are affectionately known throughout the Borders. Despite the removal of the garrison the barracks remain the regimental headquarters to this day. Within the KOSB museum is a display of regimental items and honours won by its serving members throughout the regiment's existence. Included is the VC won by Piper Daniel Laidlaw, one of the best-known World War I heroes of the Borders who, at the Battle of Loos in World War I, although wounded and in the face of a mustard gas attack, continued to pipe his companions forward into action.

The citation reads:

> For most conspicuous bravery prior to an assault on German trenches near Loos and hill 70 on the 25th of September 1915. During the first of the bombardment when the attack was about to commence Piper Laidlaw, seeing that his Company was somewhat shaken by the effect of gas, with absolute coolness and disregard to his own danger, went to the parapet, marched up and down, and played his Company out of the trench. The effect of his splendid example was immediate. The Company dashed out to the assault, Piper Laidlaw continued playing despite being wounded.

Daniel Laidlaw is buried in the churchyard at Norham a few miles upriver on the Tweed.

The KOSB museum includes souvenirs and weapons garnered in the many campaigns from the Boer War to Northern Ireland, where the regiment has served with distinction. Two rooms are dedicated to life-like tableaus. That of the officer's mess, brightly lit and formal in stark contrast to the World War II standing patrol at Maas River in Holland. Dim and eerie, some members of the patrol are brewing up over a 'tommy cooker' in what appears to be an old cattle shed or stable. A shadowy figure stands watch over the marsh lit by the flashes of gunfire, the soldiers' conversation punctuated by the noise of battle. Even the air permutes the aroma of bog and marsh; it is extremely authentic.

Throughout the recruitment area of the KOSB the towns have granted the 'freedom' to their regiment: Stranraer, Wigtown, Dumfries, Selkirk, Kirkcudbright and Sanquhar, all Royal Burghs; Melrose, Hawick, Duns, Newtown Stewart and

Coldstream all either Burghs of Barony or Police Burghs prior
to 1975.

Freedom charters are displayed in a room containing a model
of the Battle of Minden, where the regiment fought on I August
1759 and where it attained its second battle honour when still
known as the 25th Edinburgh Regiment. It was from here that
the tradition of wearing a rose on the 1st of August (Minden
Day) originated.

Also within the barracks is the display, 'By Beat of the Drum'
charting the progress of the British Army from the time of
Cromwell to Colonial days. Berwick's own museum is situated
within the gymnasium block, giving a life-like display of the
town in past times.

The museum also carries a selection of artifacts and art
treasures donated by Sir William Burrel, who spent his retire-
ment at Hutton Castle in Berwickshire. Sir William did not
donate his entire collection of works of art and bric a brac to
his native city of Glasgow where the famous Burrel collection
is now housed in a purpose-built museum. Some he gave to
Berwick on Tweed. In the 1930s a horse and cart drew up
outside the small museum at Berwick on Tweed and 185 works
of art from around the world were carefully unloaded — a gift
to the town from Sir William Burrel. During the next twenty
years, until his death in 1958, the eccentric William called
regularily at the museum, and pulling from under his coat
yet another priceless object, he would present it to the town.
In all, the shipping magnate donated over 800 items, a tenth
of his entire collection to the town.

Conventional displays are used for some of Berwick's Burrel
collection, but there is also the trial of the dragon, the viewer
passing through the twisting mock dragon inset windows to
view some of the oriental pieces. A 'bazaar scene' captures the
atmosphere of Cairo in brassware and Arab weaponry.

Modern-day Berwick on Tweed forms one of the principal
shopping centres in the Borders, drawing people in from
around a 25-mile radius. Street markets are held in Marygate
every Wednesday and Saturday, providing an extra attraction
for shoppers in search of bargains. Once an important event
in the hiring of farmworkers, Berwick Fair is held at the
end of May in Marygate, but the days are long gone when

a ploughman engaged for employment with the shake of the hand.

Coastal trading effort moved from Berwick the quayside to the Tweed Dock on the south side of the river when the basin was completed in 1877. Grain products are the principal cargoes handled at Tweed Dock with a regular traffic in barley, both inward and outward, and oil seed, rape and malted barley from Simpson's Tweedmouth works. Cement for the Border's area was, prior to the opening of the Dunbar cement works, another regular import, a trade now reversed as Dunbar cement forms an export cargo for the Shetland Islands and north-east Scotland.

Berwick's fishing fleet can also be found at Tweed Dock, but it consists solely of small vessels engaged in crab and lobster fishing or sea angling. Rough ground, in layman's terms a rocky sea bed, extends in places up to four miles offshore from Berwick and forms an ideal habitat for crustacea.

This same ground, impossible to trawl, forms a haven for sea fish, with codling being the predominant species. Angling parties travel from all around Britain to sample the sport often concentrated on Spittal Hirst, a pinnacle rising to 30ft below the surface some four miles offshore.

Salmon netting, with which Berwick has strong associations, has suffered a decline since 1989, when the netting rights owned by the Berwick Salmon Fisheries Company were sold off to the Atlantic Salmon Preservation Trust, a body backed by river angling interests. Berwick Salmon Fisheries Company, which continues to operate under new management from premises at Sandstell Road, Spittal was founded in 1764 as the Berwick Shipping Company, whose main trade involved carrying Tweed salmon to the London markets. Originally this was cured with salt and spices before being packed in barrels something similar to salted herrings. When it was realized that the use of ice could deliver salmon to London more or less fresh this latter method was adopted.

Netting stations remaining in operation can be found on the lower estuary between Carr Rock pier and the sea. They provide a constant attraction to visitors and at least seasonal employment for the crew. Salmon netting on the Tweed has always been restricted to a net and cobble fishery, no fixed engines or traps being allowed, which means that even with the sweep nets in accustomed use these must be kept moving at all times.

Once the netting season opened in bitter mid-February, when upstream at Norham a special service was held at midnight on opening day to bless the nets for the coming months, fishermen enduring some bleak conditions on the wind, rain, sleet and snow swept banks. A scarcity of spring salmon, once the mainstay of the river, has caused the opening date to be postponed until mid-April in an effort to allow more springers to escape.

Alongside the official salmon-netting business runs its unofficial shadow, conducted with some degree of enthusiasm along the lower river, despite the presence of the headquarters of the bailiff force of the River Tweed Commissioners in Tweedmouth. Such has been the intensity of what almost amounts to open warfare that these headquarters in Berwick were literally burned to the ground in an arson attack, which, along with assaults upon individual bailiffs' property, if anything lost any local support the poachers liked to claim.

From Tweedmouth the superintendent in charge of the bailiff force must endeavour to supervise not only the eighty miles or so of the Tweed up to Peebles, but also the myriad of tributary streams which include all those in Northumbria, as the entire Tweed system is subject to Scottish law — Not to mention the entire sea area up to five miles offshore from Cockburnspath to Emmanual Head on Holy Island.

New legislation and modern equipment have helped the bailiff force to eliminate much of the daylight poaching which once took place on the estuary where the ongauns made something of a spectator sport while fish were running during the autumn months. Unbridled by regulation the clandestine salmon-catching industry would be free to use any productive method appropriate to the prevailing conditions. In practice only two are in popular use, there is in fact some pride in the job, one well known poacher of large physical dimensions has been heard to promise a dire fate upon, 'ony bugger he finds poisioning or blasting his river'.

Crude methods such as the cleek — a barbed gaff, or sniggling — foul hooking, are little used on the lower river, more subtle methods being employed. Most usual is the 'chuckie in net' a few yards of monofilament nylon net weighted with a half brick on the lower end and buoyed by a lemonade bottle half filled with water on the upper.

This is your 'fixed engine'; of course it must be set in a 'good stand' where fish run close to the bank, or where a suitable eddy might keep it fishing throughout a tide. Productive stands are common knowledge to poachers and bailiffs, the latter having been known to lie in wait to ensnare the former as they arrive to collect the fruits of their efforts.

Brayer souls shun the 'chuckie in', opting instead for the dinghy method, and what a dinghy to launch forth on great waters! A tractor or lorry tyre inflated around a canvas can only be described as something of a frail craft, employed to tow out a length of netting to encircle running salmon or hang static to act as a gill or an entangling net.

Many people from throughout the eastern part of Berwickshire find employment in Berwick. Three major firms provide the focus. Jus Rol, 'Makers of the original puff pastry' are one of the success stories on Tweedside Trading Estate. From a small family bakery in Coldstream run by the late Tommy Forsyth, Jus Rol, now part of an international company, has grown into a market leader in frozen foods with a wide range of products.

Pringle of Scotland are another success story on the Tweedside Trading Estate. While much of the knitwear industry suffered recession in the early 1990s, Hawick-based Pringles, through investment in computerised knitting machines, and by producing a quality product, have remained bouyant.

On the same trading estate the Simpson's Maltings transform barley form throughout the Borders and Europe into the basic ingredient for the brewing and distilling industries. Other grain dealing enterprises are found at Tweedside and on the North Road Industrial Estate.

Turning to sporting activities, Berwick Rangers, the local team, are to be found playing in — yes — the Scottish League! Usually the second division, but for one heady season achieved first division status. Visiting teams, some of whose names are bywords in Scottish footballing circles, have departed north after playing Berwick Rangers in a Cup Final tie well and truly trounced:

Berwick Rangers (D. Smith Photo Centre)

In their black and gold,
This 'C' team so bold,
Beat Dundee division 'B'.

These words were penned by an enthusiastic local scribe in the local press and sung to the tune of 'Wonderful, wonderful Copenhagen' on the occasion in the 1950s when Berwick Rangers beat Dundee in a Scottish Cup Tie played at the old Shiefield Stadium. The team's giant killing exploits include knocking the more famous Glasgow Rangers out of the Scottish Cup — an occasion which will never be forgotten by the core of fans who through thick and thin give the Black and Golds loyal unbridled support.

That then is a brief look at Berwick upon Tweed, a town with a unique history. Is it Scottish, English, or simply Berwick? More than anything else the last would be the best description. The intermix between the town and Berwickshire continue to this day. Despite Berwick being over the Border in England and Northumberland it is the natural focal point for employment, sport, recreation and business for many people of the Merse.

116

# CHAPTER 5

# Kelso to St Boswells

There's a fine auld toon in the Borderland,
By the sides o' the silvery Tweed,
Where the salmon leap on the silver strand,
And the game and the cattle feed.

That's Kelso, one of the fairest of all Border towns standing above the joining of Tweed and Teviot. The name Kelso is said to be derived from chalk ridge, once Calchow or Kelkow locally; today always known as Kelsae. Few towns anywhere, be it in the Borders or beyond, can boast such a fine example of a small-town market square. Indeed throughout Britain as a whole that of Kelso's Market Square would be difficult to surpass.

Kelsae's song continues.

Then let us all wi' heart and voice,
Sing the praises o' Kelsae's name,
We will work and play and aye rejoice,
That Kelsae is oor hame.

The whinstone setts or cobbles which form the surface may be cursed by the motorist but are easier on the eye than the smoothest of tarmacadam. Several streets radiating from the square also retain this surface which seems capable of withstanding even the most severe abuse which modern traffic places upon the cobbles.

Two buildings, the one-time Town Hall, built in 1816 on the site of a former tollbooth, and the Cross Keys Hotel, dominate the square, while the majority of the surrounding businesses are small family concerns, their shop fronts retaining this individuality. As yet the multi-national companies have not been allowed to create their mayhem within Kelsae Square.

Set among the Square's cobblestones the bullring marks the place where once stood the pride of Border sires. Markets have long since ceased to be held in the town centre, but the

Kelso Square

surrounding streets of Horse, Coal and Wood Markets bear witness to the trades once carried out in the town centre.

Cattle were still being traded in Kelso's streets up until the 1930s, while across the river Tweed the annual St James' Fair held on 5th August was an important business and social occasion. These events are long gone from Kelso, with the Border Union Agricultural Society Show in July forming a replacement for the old Fair.

Before the Royal Highland Show obtained its permanent site at Ingliston, Kelso was one of the venues on the 'Highlands' travels, having been last held here in the 1950s. The Border Union, or rather Kelsae Show at Springwood Park remains an annual event every July.

For a local show Kelso is held in some esteem, attracting a wide range of machinery exhibitors. It has varied ring events and is referred to as the 'wee Highland'. Traders stands today have extended from farm machinery to include clothing and gardening, estate agents and art, together with everything a horse or horse owner could desire.

Kelso Abbey


A Friday and Saturday two-day event, the ring events on Fridays are mainly equestrian, but Saturday sees a parade of livestock and at least one spectacular event such as giant car crushing trucks. Events at Springwood Park bring a flow of visitors to Kelso over the year and include ram and horse sales plus a major dog show.

Further attractions for visitors to Kelso can be found in the racecourse, which also features a Sunday Market, and the ice rink, where curling and skating take place during the winter months.

Kelso Civic Week is a fairly recent festival, but adopts many of the features of the older Common Ridings. The main event is the Kelsae Laddie leading the cavalcade of followers on rideouts to neighbouring villages. The ride to Yetholm on the final Saturday of the celebrations is the major event of Kelso Civic Week, taking a circular course to Yetholm and returning by Linton and Bowmont Forest.

Kelso never had a dependency on the wool trade as is found in other Border towns. Writing in *The Statistical Account of*

Over the jumps Border Union Show Kelso

*Scotland 1791–99*, Dr Christopher Douglas bemoans the lack of industry in the town despite sitting amidst a plentiful supply of raw material:

> 'Coal is brought from a greater distance, and sold at a higher price, than in Kelso, yet in these towns they flourish, and are carried on to a considerable extent.'

There were, however, 147 shoemakers at the time far surpassing those employed in any other trade, who turned out annually 30,000 pairs of shoes and up to 400 pairs of boots. At the same time Christopher bemoans the fact that the skinners who would have supplied the shoemakers leather were in the habit of drying hides in the churchyard. Enough said, Christopher, to make the very swine turn in their graves!

A skinner's yard features as one of the displays in Kelso's museum, and there is an information room in the Turret House at Abbey Court immediately opposite Kelso Abbey.

There is also a Victorian school room complete with squeaky slates, artifacts from around Kelso and from Roxburgh Castle a selection of exquisitely wrought stone arrow heads.

Sitting at the confluence of Tweed and one of its major tributaries it is little wonder that Kelso is a town of anglers. The Junction Pool where Teviot joins Tweed is perhaps one of the most photographed salmon beats in the British Isles. It is also one of the most productive pools during the peak season where, fish wait to run the cauld, the place where Micheal Scott bade his assistant girdle the Tweed with stone.

Within striking distance are the famous beats of Upper, Middle and Lower Floors, Henderside, and Rutherford. At some twenty miles upstream the river is an ideal distance from the sea for salmon angling. Fish are still fresh — a term applied to salmon not long out of salt water — and, most importantly for the angler, thinking of pausing in their dash to the headwaters and likely to take an anglers fly or other offering.

It is little wonder, with such a proliferation of angling, that Kelso was at one time an important centre for tackle manufacture. Two firms were involved, the history of both being today rather sketchy. Extensive premises were occupied behind the Square on either side of Roxburgh Street. Today both these firms, Forrest and Redpath, can still be found in the town although no members of the original families are involved in their running. Nor is any manufacturing carried out; like other rural fishing-tackle dealers Forrest and Redpath are retail outlets only.

Before regionalisation in the 1970s Kelso had one of the most progressive town councils in the Borders, being active campaigners for new jobs and businesses in the town. Now established are firms manufacturing plastic goods and high quality sound-recording equipment, supplementing the old firms of agricultural engineers and soft drinks manufacturers.

The cauld referred to earlier in this chapter once drove millwheels for Hogarth's a long established firm dealing in grain products. Water power may be long redundant but Hogarth's remain in operation producing animal feedstuffs, oatmeal, porridge oats and pearl barley. This latter is a familiar ingredient in Scotch broth and only uses barley of the very highest quality, mainly grown around the Borders.

Perhaps in the twelfth century, when Kelso Abbey was founded, the Tironension monks appreciated salmon as part of their diet, especially during the days and seasons when consumption of other flesh was forbidden. Kelso was the first of the Border Abbeys to be founded by the 'sair Saint' David I having assisted the establishment of Kelso in AD 1128

Originally the Order had been set up at Selkirk in 1113, but moved to Kelso about 1126–28 bringing it close to the royal burgh and castle of Roxburgh across Tweed and Teviot. Not that this proved to be of any protection, as attacks upon the Abbey were frequent occurrences. During the Wars of Independence Kelso, like the other Border Abbeys, suffered severely from the English invaders, the building being abandoned for a period in 1296.

Strife continued around Kelso Abbey almost throughout its active history. Invasions by Darce and Surrey brought violence upon the Abbey's walls, the final blow coming from Hereford's 1545 punitive blow on behalf of Henry VIII. Artillery breached the walls after the surviving defenders fought a last ditch stand in the tower — a brief act of final defiance before they were finally overrun and slain.

Following the death of James II his infant son was crowned King James III in the Abbey in 1460. Before its final destruction, when reformers in 1547 completed the work of centuries of warfare, Kelso rose to be one of the wealthiest monastic establishments in the land. Eventually the presence of the Abbey brought Kelso to prominence over the old town of Roxburgh as the new town sprang up around the Abbey walls. A description by John Duncan in 1517 includes a note that the majority of Kelso's inhabitants were then employed or beholden to the Abbey in some way or another.

Today the remains of Kelso Abbey are more sparse than those of its counterparts, and yet the gaunt west transept with its Gallilee porch gives an indication of its past grandeur.

Spanning Tweed a short distance from Kelso Abbey is the graceful five-arch bridge designed by John Rennie, whose construction was completed in 1756. From Maxwellheugh on the south bank Rennie's bridge provides a foreground for one of the finest views of Kelso, with Abbey and church spires prominent over the old part of the town. Kelso Bridge is said to have been a prototype for Rennie's London Waterloo Bridge, built in 1817 and since demolished. A toll house associated with the bridge still stands on the upstream north bank, the deeply etched cut in the parapet is said to have been caused by generations of toll payers scoring their fee along the bridge prior to paying. A bypass, including a new bridge, is under planning consideration for Kelso, hopefully to relieve the town centre and the old bridge from the pressure of through traffic.

On a high grassy mound betwixt Tweed and Teviot a few fingers of crumbling stone mark the once Royal Castle of Roxburgh's position. The site is a natural one for defence with Teviot tight below the south wall. Further protection to the north comes from a now dry moat alongside the Kelso-St Boswells road.

Despite the scant remains, Roxburgh, with its Royal Burgh — of which nothing remains on the ground — played a major role in the history of Scotland. So important was the settlement that a mint was established in the burgh and coins are some of the few relics of its former greatness. Alexander III was born at Roxburgh Castle, and it was one of the favourite residences of David I, where he is said to have formulated his plans for the four great Border abbeys.

Lying so close to English territory it is not surprising that Roxburgh Castle was the scene of many disputes and of actual changes of ownership between Scots and English. Despite being in Scotland, Roxburgh Castle was English and was held for 160 years, from around AD 1300.

During one of these periods of English occupation it is said that a band led by the 'Black Douglas' — Sir James — had crept below the castle walls covered in cattle skins. Sentries ignored the dark shapes below the walls, since they were accustomed to the movement of cattle in the dusk. Walls were scaled unseen and, according to legend, the first sign of intrusion came when Sir James tapped a soldier's wife on the shoulder. Naturally the lady had been crooning a lullaby to the child she cradled:

Hush yet, hush ye, little pet ye,
Hush ye, hush ye, do not fret ye,
The Black Douglas shall not get ye.

From the darkness behind her the voice of Sir James is said to have replied, 'I'm not so sure of that'. Or so at least the story goes.

While laying siege to Roxburgh castle in 1460 King James II's interest in artillery led to his untimely death. 'The Lion', a siege piece similar to the famous Mons Meg (which can still be seen at Edinburgh Castle) exploded, killing the king outright. His young son was crowned James III at Kelso Abbey while a holly tree across the river in the grounds of Floors Castle marks the spot where the incident occurred.

The loss of their king in such tragic circumstances brought a decrease in enthusiams among the nobles for pursuing the siege. James's widow rallied the cause when, despite her grief she pointed out that the king was but one man while his army was many, and that a new king would soon be produced, as at least a figurehead for the cause. Hence the rapid arrival of her son in Kelso to be crowned James III of Scotland. Thereafter the siege continued, with the ultimate capture and destruction of Roxburgh Castle, so long a thorn in the side of Scotland and a refuge for the enemy almost in the heart of the Borders.

Enjoying a sunny aspect amid extensive parkland, Floors Castle is the ducal seat of the Dukes of Roxburghe, the Innes Kers, descendants of the Kers of Cessford. The original tower of the Kers stands above the Cessford Burn on a broad ridge where the views extend around Teviotdale and beyond to the Cheviots. Cattle now graze peacefully around the cracked crumbling tower of Cessford Castle, and there is little to indicate that here was the stronghold of one of the most active of the reiving families of the sixteenth century.

English Wardens of the Middle march had cause for continued complaint about the activities of some of the Cessford Kers. As if this was not enough they engaged in family feuds involving other Border families, or they quarrelled with the other branch of the Kerr clan who spelt their name with a double r, with whom there was continual rivalry about the wardenship of the Scottish Middle March. It was with the Scott's of Buccleuch that one of the longest running Ker feuds took place, culminating in the murder of Scott of Buccleuch in the High Street of Edinburgh with the assistance of a party of the Hume clan.

Floors Castle Kelso home of the Duke of Roxburghe

The mansion of Floors dates from 1721. It is thought to have been designed and built by Sir John Vanburgh for the first Duke of Roxburghe. More recent research seems to indicate that the present centre block formed the eighteenth century building, credit for the design being given to William Adam, father of Robert, for what was then a plain Georgian country house. Reconstruction took place in the early nineteenth century, around 1839, when the 6th Duke engaged W. H. Playfair as architect to add the two wings and the extensive decoration, as is seen at Floors Castle today, creating what can only be described as an exotic roofscape equal to or surpassing any in Scotland.

Floors Castle is open to the public for the months between Easter and October, when both house and policies can be viewed. Art treasures abound within Floors. One of the best examples is claimed to be the fifteenth-century Brussels tapestry hung in the anteroom, which represents in unusually fine weave 'The Day of the Pentecost' and 'The Descent of the Holy Ghost.' Tapestries are very much a theme at Floors Castle, including a

Cessford Castle

set in the drawing room specially created by the 8th Duchess in Louis XV style to accommodate 'The Triumphs of the Gods'. Naturally the furnishings match the magnificence of the wall hangings, including a Louis XV marquetry cabinet by Latz. The list continues through the needle room, and the ballroom to the bird room, containing a vast collection of stuffed birds, some now extremely rare, or, like the example of the passenger pigeon, extinct. Fossils and minerals, together with a display of artifacts collected by the Roxburghe family are on view.

During the summer months the grounds of Floors Castle form the venue for a number of events, some of a charitable nature, from waupenschaus to hunter trials. After two days' heavy rain the 1988 game fair of the Scottish Landowners Federation, the major event of the sporting year, was a somewhat muddy affair. The haugh where the unfortunate James II met his end rapidly became a quagmire, churned into a sea of mud by the 100,000 crowd who attended the event, and cars were being towed *into* car parks!

Kelso was a major influence in the life of Sir Walter Scoot; at Rosebank, the home of his paternal bachelor uncle Robert Scott and his sister Jenny, he spent part of his early years. Here, while attending the old Grammar School in the shadow of the Abbey, Scott first made the aquaintance of the Ballantyne brothers, James and John, who were to figure prominently in his later life.

John Ballantyne became established as a printer and publisher in Kelso, where from the premises of the *Kelso Mail* in 1799 he published the first of Scott's works, *An Apology for Tales of Terror*. This was the foundation of the Ballantyne Press, from which issued in 1802 the first two volumes of *Minstrelsy of the Scottish Border*. With an injection of £5,000 Scott joined James Ballantyne on their first joint publishing venture in 1805. This was Scott's first venture into the publishing world, leading to financial collapse in 1826. With £120,000 owing Scott set about its repayment in the only way he knew, by writing. This excessive labour, it is said, resulted in ill-health and his early death in an effort to repay his creditors.

Scott's earlier association with the Borders began in 1733 at the age of three, when, as a sickly child he was sent to his grandparents' home at Sandyknowe near the village of Smailholm, a few miles north of Kelso. Here it was felt that the fresh air and plain food would protect young-Scott from the fate of his six siblings who had died in early childhood. Coddled by his aunt Janet Walter seems to have thrived on the caller Border air. Despite the lameness of infancy, Scott in later years visited almost every historic site in the Border Country, signifying that he was an extremely physically active man. Equally important, during his sojourn at Sandyknowe his young mind was absorbing the lore of the Borderland. Verbal tales told by Sandy Ormiston, the Sandyknowe shepherd, tales from his grandparents and aunt related below the vantage point of the Smailholm Tower, were used in many of his later works. Stories of wizardry, heroes and villains, tales of spurned lovers told at a spot where many of the alleged sites of these instances could be seen, primed young Walter's imagination. Perhaps in these times the stories of witchcraft and the fairy world were believed by some of the raconteurs, making them all the more real to his young ears. Smailholm Tower, now renovated, with all floors intact, forms an appropriate display place for a tableau

Smailholm Tower

of miniature figures taken from the works of Sir Walter and traditional Border Ballads. Scottish Renaissance music plays on the first floor and the two upper walkways give superb views through the entire arc of the compass. Smailholm Tower is without doubt greatly improved from the empty dark shell of the past, especially as some of the history of the Tower can now be learned on the site.

Originally the Barony of Smailholm belonged to the Douglas family of Border fame, the Hoppringles or Pringles of Smailholm being squires of the Douglas's. After the Douglas fell from favour the Pringles continued to live at Smailholm for 200 years, eventually building Old Gala House in Galashiels — but that's a different story.

The tower of Smailholm was used by Scott in 'The Eve of St John:'

> The Baron of Smaylho'me rose with the day,
> He spurred his courser on,
> Without stop or stay, down the rocky way,
> that leads to Brotherstone.

'The Eve of St John' is a poem of the eternal triangle, mortal combat and a bit of ghostly haunting which eventually proves to much for the Baron and Lady of Smaylo'me, sending them both to take Holy Orders:

There is a Nun in Dryburgh bower,
ne'er looks upon the sun:
There is a monk in Melrose Tower,
He speaketh word to none.

That Nun who ne'er beholds the day,
That Monk, who speaks to none-
That Nun was Smaylho'me's Lady gay,
That Monk the bold baron.

Some seven miles south east of Kelso, snug against Cheviot's northern flank, are the villages of Kirk and Town Yetholm. Here The Pennine Way, Britain's oldest long-distance walk, descends from the hill ridges to its northern end at Kirk Yetholm. At the Border Hotel those who complete the walk could once claim in the bar a free half pint on the account of the late Alfred Wainwright. Officially only those who have used the Pennine Way guide book written by Wainwright are due the gratuity.

Yetholm (*yett* meaning gate in Scots) must have been subject to conflict across the Cheviot ridge into Coquetdale but little has been recorded of any such instances. From the nearby valleys of Kale and Bowmont the old Border roads Clennel Street. The Street and Dere Street offer superb walking.

Until the early years of this century Yetholm was the headquarters of many Border Gypsies, settled in the area. This concentration of travelling folk is said to have come about when the laird of Yetholm, David Bennet, granted land to gypsies who had fought alongside him with distinction at the siege of Namur in 1695. The *Statistical Account of Scotland 1791–99* gives the tinker and gypsy population of Yetholm as fifty, including women and children, all in Kirk Yetholm.

Gypsies had spread throughout Europe from the fifteenth century, the leaders of these bands giving themselves titles of kings, dukes, counts, earls and lords of Little Egypt. In Scotland as elsewhere they were subject to some persecution as, 'thievis'

Gypsy Coronation (Douglas Gibson late of G. W. Gibson Coldstream)

or, 'an infamous byke of lawless limmers', like the stragglers
who were rounded up in Haddington in 1636, when the men
were sentenced to be hanged, the women drowned, other than
those with children, who were scourged through the streets and
then burnt on the cheek.

What the Fa, Faa or Faw family left behind was the ballad of
'Johnnie Faa', a folk ballad still performed today:

> 'O come wi' me,' says Johnnie Faa,
> 'O come wi' me, my dearie;
> For I vow and swear by the hilt of my sword,
> That your lord shall nae mair come near ye.'

Kings and queen of the gypsy race were crowned at Yetholm,
their palace a simple cottage on the road to Halterburn. The
family Fa, claimed in their time to be descended from the
Egyptian Pharaohs. When the Faa line died out the gypsy
crown, a simple brass ring inset with coloured glass 'gems', fell
to Charles Blythe.

Charlie, having no male descendants, bequeathed in turn
the gypsy throne to his youngest daughter Ellen. Esther her
elder sister disputed this, the matter being settled according

to Romany custom by a wrestling bout on Yetholm green. Here Esther emerged the victor to be crowned Esther Faa Blythe Rutherford, Queen of all the gypsies in the Northern Kingdom.

Last of the gypsy line was Charles Faa Blythe, crowned in 1902 as King of Yetholm Gypsies, the last of a line and a race. Of the Yetholm gypsies only traces of their language remain, with the crowning of the barry gadgie and barry manishee (good man and good women) at the village's summer festival.

Traces of the old gypsy language still find usage not only in Yetholm but among other Border towns and villages. A language once used to deny outsiders, especially those in authority, knowledge of whatever matter was under discussion. A unique weapon, the Yetholm Jagger, once existed in Yetholm. Basically a barbed spike like a crochet hook, it was a painful instrument to be thrust into a buttock in the settlement of differences or a warning off to strangers.

Between Yetholm and Morebattle Linton Kirk sits on a pile of sand, in legend said to have been placed there as a penance by two sisters for a murder committed by their brother. In reality the sand most probably arrived because of glacial activity — a more practical but less romantic explanation. Less well known than the famous Lambton worm of Northumbria is the fearsome beast portrayed in the 'Somerville Stone' over the church door being slain by a spear-wielding horseman.

Somervilles had settled in Scotland sometime around 1136, the slaying of the beast which had its lair in the, 'Worms Hole' on Greenlees farm being credited to either William or John de Sommerville.

A large grave was discovered near Linton Kirk containing over fifty skulls, many of which bore marks of severe injury and were possibly some of the victims of Flodden.

Unclassified motor roads skirt the Cheviots through the villages of Morebattle and Hounam where it is possible for the motorist to take a shortcut to the main A 68 Carter Bar trunk road. Opting for Morebattle and Whitton Edge the views extend across much of the Border country where, between two dry stone walls, Dere Street will be seen heading southwards across moorland to climb over the Cheviots to Chew Green camp.

Linton Kirk, obviously taken from what was once a lake

At Carter Bar the modern A 68 road replaces the old Redeswire crossing between headwaters of the rivers Jed and Rede. Here on the high fells the last armed Border skirmish took place between Scots and English at what is known as the Redeswire Fray in 1575. It was the custom of these times for the Scots and English wardens of the Marches to meet at prearranged times to settle by discussion rather than by battle any differences involving the subjects under their control.

In 1575 the Scottish Warden, Sir John Carmichael, accompanied by assorted members of the Douglas, Turnbull, Elliot, Armstrong and Scott clans, met with the English warden, Sir John Forster, at Redeswire. Forster in turn had behind him a band of Fenwicks, Collingwoods and Shaftoes, who, like their Scottish counterparts, had itchy sword hands. Tempers became heated when Forster refused to hand over a noted Redesdale horse thief, one Robson who was somewhat unparticular as to whose beast stood within his stall. Words became insufficient for the expression of strong opinions with the diplomatic prattle being replaced by the metallic rattle of steel on steel. The Scots, apparently in inferior numbers, were in danger of defeat until

the timely arrival of Jedburgh's Provost Rutherford at the head
of a small band:

> Bauld, he was fou stout,
> Wi' a' his nine sons him about,
> He led the toun o' Jedburgh out,
> All Bravely fought that day.

Their assistance was enough to win the day. Over twenty of
the English party were killed with a further number of those
of high rank taken prisoner. 'Stand firm and sure for Jethart's
here', something of a motto in the town seldom referred to as
Jedburgh, but as Jeddart or Jethart.

The full ballad, 'The Raid of the Redeswire' runs to twenty
verses and begins:

> The seventh of July, the sooth to say,
> At the Reidswire the tryst was set,
> Or wardens they affixed the day,
> And, as they promised, so they met.
> Alas! That day I'll ne'er forget!
> Was sure sae feared, and then saer fain –
> Thet came ther justice for to get,
> Will never green to come again.

'The Raid of the Redeswire' is almost a blow-by-blow account
of the incident from the 'cracking crouse' (boastful talk) to the
flying arrows and hand-to-hand combat. Leading to the last
summing up verse:

> Who did invent that day of play,
> We need not fear to find him soon;
> For John Forster, I dare well say,
> Made us this noisome afternoon.
> Not that I speak precisely out,
> That he supposed it would be peril;
> But pride, and breaking out the fued,
> Gar'd Tyndale lads begin the quarrel.

The Redeswire Raid is commemorated each year in the
Jedburgh Festival led by the Jethart Callant, where at the site
of the battle an oration is given by a guest speaker. On the day
of the Redeswire Ride harassed policemen can be found making

Folk singer Ronnie Brown delivers the Redeswire oration

vain attempts to move parked motorists from the Carter Bar layby. Here, of all the three major Border Crossings, there is normally at least a place to park, viewpoint indicators, a piper and a travelling snack bar.

But back to the Jethart Festival. First-time spectators may panic and wonder how they are possibly going to be able to witness the ceremony, when for the third time the forces of the law ask them to move along. All is revealed when the first of Jethart's citizens arrive to open a rather rickety gate, whereupon what seems half the population of the Borders drives into the bumpy field to set up picnic tables and await the arrival of the cavalcade.

By 11.30 the riders are in sight as the crowd gathers behind Redeswire Stane which commemorates the event: 'On this ridge on July 7th 1575 was fought one of the last Border frays known as the Raid of Redeswire'. The string of riders vanishes into a hollow where first to reappear is the red-coated Herald and the Jethart Callant. Their horses are put to a gallop up the ridge to where the crowd has gathered, where, as he passes, the Callant gives the stirring cry of 'Jetharts here!'

At Redeswire in 1991 Scotland's best known folk-singer, Ronnie Brown, late of the Corries, gave the oration which was not only apt to Jedburgh, the Borders and Scotland, but was also amusing. A few words from the Jethart Callant and then the Jethart song of pride and defiance:

The cry's gone through the Borderland,
The beacons blaze on the Dunion top,
Thae English knaves frae Cumberland,
Ha' crossed the fell by Cairter's Slap.
Dear Borderland blanch not nor fear,
Oor Borderland nae foe come near,
Stand firm and sure for Jethart's here,
Stand firm and sure for Jethart's here.

Other rideouts in the Jethart Festival Week include following part of the route taken by Mary Queen of Scots on her epic ride to visit Lord Bothwell at Hermitage Castle in Liddesdale.

From the Carter Bar the A68 shares the Jed valley a few miles downstream from its source. Sir Dick Lauder, writing in the 19th century, cited these headwaters of the Jed as one of the few places in the Borders where vestiges of the old Caledonian Forest could still be seen. The Capon Tree, an ancient oak supported by poles, stands lower downstream, the doleful survivor of the once extensive Jed Forest.

Here at Carter Bar the Wauchope Forest forms the edge of one of the largest areas of man-made woodlands in Britain. Extending south into the Kielder and Wark forests towards Hadrian's Wall, the almost unbroken ranks of trees reach west to beyond Newcastleton in Liddesdale.

A short distance from the A68 can be found the Jedforest Deer and Farm Park. Here is the only opportunity in the Borders to see red deer in the farm's domesticated herd where the red deer form Britain's newest farm animal. A collection of farm animals of the past are included at the Park, which incorporates woodland walks and children's play areas.

James Thompson, author of *The Seasons*, although born at Ednam near Kelso, spent his young life at Southdean beside the Jed where its course curves back from Chesters to the A68. While Thompson's 'Seasons' are all but forgotten he is perhaps best remembered as the author of 'Rule Britannia'.

Downstream, opposite Jedburgh, where the Jed has cut into
bank and scaur, the old red sandstone lies exposed. Many miles
downstream on Tweedside those who work on the river will tell
at a glance whether a flash spate has come from Tweeddale, or
if the red colour is pronounced it means that it is from Jed
through Teviot that the flood waters have come.

Of all Border towns Jedburgh, more than any other, is well
situated and convenient to the car-borne visitor. Adjacent to
where the busy A68 skirts the town beside the River Jed, a
spacious car park and the largest tourist information centre
in the Borders are but a few minutes walk from the main
attractions of the town.

Grouped within a small area are Queen Mary's House, the
Market Square, and of course the ruins of Jedburgh's Abbey
Church. Overlooking the lower part of the town, the ruins,
lacking only a roof stand almost as complete as when the last
canons departed in the mid-sixteenth century. Gone are the
ancillary buildings providing accommodation and storage and
the mill also, although the dry water-supplying lade remains,
as do the foundations of the outlying buildings.

Entering through a visitor centre a video film is available on
the Abbey, and upstairs some of the artifacts recovered in past
excavations may be seen. A model of the complete settlement as
it was in its heyday sits before a large window overlooking the
ruins and the figure of an Augustinian friar watches over all.

The settlement at Jedburgh of a group of Augustinian canons
dates to around 1138 when they arrived from France under
the patronage of King David I. Originally dedicated as a
priory, Jedburgh was raised to abbey status sixteen years
later, and became one of the most important religious houses
in Scotland.

The construction of Jedburgh's Abbey spanned almost one
hundred years and is today considered to be one of the
best surviving examples of a great Scottish abbey church of
the Gothic period. During the time taken over construction
styles changed with a marked contrast between the heavy
Romanesque style of the choir against the light airy earlier
Gothic nave.

One of the notable occasions around this period at Jedburgh
was the wedding of King Alexander III to Yoland de Dreux

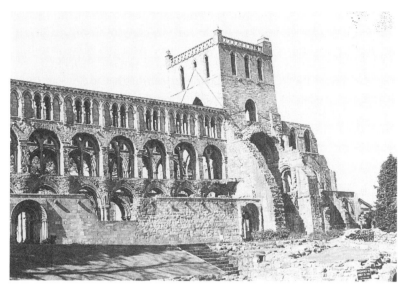

Jedburgh Abbey

in 1285. According to tradition the celebrations following the marriage were disrupted by the appearance of a spectre in the shape of Death. To the superstitious people of that time what could have been an illusion by a clever entertainer was regarded as an ill omen. Whatever the truth of the matter Alexander died below the cliffs at Kinghorn in Fife the following year, leaving Scotland's future dependent upon the fragile Maid of Norway.

Little else has been recorded concerning the early years of Jedburgh Abbey. Life seems to have been reasonably peaceful up until 1297 when soldiers of Edward I's army ransacked the building, stripping the lead covering from the roof. Around forty seems to have been the maximum number of canons at Jedburgh — a peak reached in the early thirteenth century, whereafter monastic activity began to decline.

The years 1410, 1416 and 1464 seem to have brought serious assault upon the abbey, which by 1502 was being described as ruinous. Something worthy of despoliation must have remained, as Surrey found enough to burn in 1523, setting the scene for further destruction in the rough wooing of Henry VIII in 1544 and 1545.

Reformers brought about the final demise of monastic life at Jedburgh Abbey which was finally suppressed in 1559, although the Abbey Church continued to be used as a place of worship until 1875, when it was replaced by a new parish church.

Only eight miles from the Border, Jedburgh Castle was such a magnet for attack that its walls were flung down by the Scots themselves in 1409. On more or less the same site above Castlegate the present building, still known as 'the castle' is in fact the only surviving example of a nineteenth-century Howard Reform Prison last used as a jail in 1886. This building was designed in 1820 by Arthur Elliot who was born in nearby Ancrum. Elliot trained as a joiner, but after a disagreement with the architect during the renovations of Douglas Castle in Lanarkshire he took over the completion of the work successfully and went on to become a leading Scottish architect. In the Borders his work includes Stobo Castle in Peebleshire, Minto House in Roxburghshire and the Haining in Selkirk.

The 'Castle' hosts a museum to the life of Jedburgh in the past as well as a glimpse of a Reform Prison where the bill of fare hardly makes mouth-watering reading. Breakfast: 2 pints oatmeal porridge with a half pennyworth of milk, with the same menu for supper; 2 pints of broth containing barley, meat and vegetables and a penny roll for dinner.

Also seen here are some of Jedburgh's past trades, including the North British Rayon Mill once the principal employer in the town. A factory producing artificial silk opened in 1928 and closed with devastating effects in 1956. Not that it was a healthy place to work among acids capable of burning hands, and it was only after some battle that North British supplied rubber gloves for their employees. Factory conditions were such, through the emission of toxic fumes from the process, that two pints of milk were given to workers on each shift to counteract the effect of chemicals upon their stomachs.

Here we learn that the town was once famous for its pears. 'Jetthart Pears' was a common street call of London Hawkers in the eighteenth century, the town being at that time famous for its orchards and the variety and quality of its pears. Pears originated with the French Augustinian monks who founded the Abbey in the 12th century. By the 1700s much of Jedburgh was covered by orchards of which a survivor can be seen to this day in the Friars' gardens, still bearing excellent fruit.

Peculiar to some Borders towns are sweets, manufactured on a small scale and with a local connection. Jedburgh is no exception, where Irene Miller of Miller's a fruit and vegetable shop still makes the unique 'Jethart Snails.' Assisted by her son Rutherford, Irene manufactures on a small scale what she says are about the only commercially hand-produced sweets in Britain. Jethart Snails have a light minty flavour, the recipe having been given to the Miller family more than a hundred years ago by a Napoleonic French prisoner of war.

If the story of 'Jethart justice', the act of hanging a wrongdoer and conducting the trial later, were true, there would have been little call for prison or prisoners. Possibly the saying has nothing to do with the citizens of Jedburgh, but relates instead to the execution without trial of Borderers in the reign of James VI.

While the castle may be gone Queen Mary's House still remains, where that unfortunate lady recovered from an illness incurred during her ride from Hermitage back to Jedburgh. Later, when incarcerated by her cousin in England, Queen Mary is said to have regretted not 'having died at Jedwort'. The house is a fine example of a restored town house and today acts as a museum to Queen Mary and her association with the Borders. On display are a number of items associated with Queen Mary including her death mask, tapestry and communion set. Her watch was recovered near Hawick in 1817 within the soil flung up by a burrowing mole. A few years ago the watch was stolen from the museum but was returned anonymously some time later, leading to an improved security system on all exhibits.

Within the building spiral stairs have a left-hand twist, a legacy of the original owners, the family Kerr. 'Kery' or 'cary' handed is a common term applied to left-handed people. The left-hand twist on the stairs enabled them to be more easily defended by a left-handed swordsman.

Talking of Kerrs, the Ferniehirst branch branch of the family were sometimes at odds with the citizens of Jedburgh, especially in the time of Mary Queen of Scots, when Sir Thomas Kerr of Ferniherst and Scott of Buccleuch were in favour of the Queen, while Jedburgh supported her son, later to be James VI.

With a force of 3,000 men, including some English banditti, Kerr and Buccleuch planned to put Jedburgh to the torch in February 1572. Not that the citizens of Jeddart were going to allow them free entry, as the town stood to arms, and the messenger who brought a letter from the opposition was forced to dine upon the same. Assistance arrived in the shape of government support from Edinburgh when aided by the Kers of Cessford and the Jeddart people the would be attackers were seen off the premises. Eventually by 1581 the differences between Ferniherst and Jedburgh were patched up as in this year Sir Thomas Kerr was provost of the burgh.

For a period of twenty-five years from 1523 Ferniehirst was held by an English garrison who treated the local populace, with a severe degree of brutality. Sir John Kerr, son of Sir Andrew or 'Dand' Kerr, a notable character, recaptured Ferniehirst with the assistance of a French force in 1548.

Revenge was as equally savage as the atrocities commited by the garrison, who attempted to save themselves by surrendering to the French rather than to the bloodthirsty locals. So desperate were the Scots upon vengence that captured weapons were traded with the French for their prisoners, who were promptly slain or slowly 'pricked' to death by the mounted spearsmen.

Jedburgh's 'Ba Game' where the Doonies, those below the Market Square, and the Uppies, from above, strive to pass a leather ball over the opposing goals, is said to have originated from this battle at Ferniehirst when the game was played with the heads of the slain English. Jed Water joins Teviot a half mile or so downstream of Monteviot House, family home of the Marquis of Lothian who is descended from the Ferniherst Kerrs.

At Monteviot the Woodland Visitor Centre gives an insight into the world of trees, plants and the uses of timber on a large and small scale. Almost a full day is required for a proper visit to the Woodland Centre if the estate walks are to be included.

The Centre itself consists of renovated buildings, where, among other things, can be traced the history of plant collection, especially that of the Veitch family who originated in Jedburgh. Founded by John Veitch (1752–1839) who removed to Devon, through five generations, until 1949, when the last of the line died out in Ann Mildred Veitch, the family were prominent plant collectors scouring the far corners of the globe for new specimens. Within the centre can be found many examples of the woodworker's art in turning and the making of small items. Should you think that the modern child must have something which bleeps and flashes, take a trip upstairs at the Centre. Up here all is silent except the click of wood upon wood, as children of all ages up to at least sixty, strive to solve problems created in wood. Occasional a scream may rend the air as the deceptively simple cats-cradle affair, where the problem of bringing two wooden balls threaded on string together over a wooden bar, defeats yet another visitor. No, you cannot take that one home to solve the problem, but smaller versions are available in the shop downstairs.

Four walks may be enjoyed from the Woodland Centre, all colour-coded and easiest to follow. One is even suitable for wheelchairs, but the best is the longest. This, the 'green' walk, winds through woodland, sometimes mature old beeches and other hardwoods, at others alongside evergreen plantations. The destination is Peniel Heugh, and the Wellington Monument, taking in a total distance of some four miles.

Nowhere can the going be described as strenuous, sometimes by path, sometimes by forestry road leading upwards to the tower of the Wellington Monument, where a plaque reads, 'To the Duke of Wellington and the British Army, William Kerr VI Marquis of Lothian and his Tenantry dedicated this monument'.

Cut from the Cheviots by Teviotdale, overlooking the Tweed valley, the views from Peniel Heugh are stupendous, encompassing the entire Borderland from the Cheviot Hills, west to the Eildons, around the rim of the Lammermuirs to the distant sea coast. Unfortunately the monument itself is closed because of its poor state of repair, but from the top the view must even surpass that from the crag.

The Wellington Walk is circular, returning downhill to join the tarred roads within Monteviot policies, where an extension may be made to other coded walks as their markers are encountered.

Within the policies surrounding Monteviot the line of Dere Street has been lost, the one-time branch railway to Jedburgh having assisted the obliteration. North of Teviot the line

Peniel Heugh one of the walks from the Monteviot Woodland Centre

appears again to rise over Ancrum Moor by Lilliards Edge, named after Maiden Lilliard of Maxton who, despite fearful wounds, is said to have fought courageously at the Battle of Ancrum Moor in 1545.

A monument marking the grave of Lilliard sits on the ridge on the line of Dere Street half a mile east of the A68. On the surrounding wall are a few lines, 'To all true Scotsmen, by me its been mendit'.

A further line is indecipherable.

The main inscription reads:

Fair Maiden Lilliard
Lies under this stane;
Little was her stature,
But Muckle was her fame.
Upon the English loons
She laid many thumps,
And when her legs were cuttit off
She fought upon her stumps.

Fought in 1545, Ancrum Moor was one of the last battles between Scots and English. Under Sir Ralph Evers and Sir Brian Laiton the English army had despoiled the Scottish Borders as far north as Melrose. Among other acts they defaced the Douglas Tombs in Melrose Abbey and were returning south with their spoils when they were engaged by the Scots, commanded by the Earl of Angus and Scott of Buccleuch.

A feint of a retreat was made by the Scottish army, but this was merely to select their own ground where the invaders lost 800 hundred dead including their commanders and a 1,000 taken prisoner. Mixed up in this battle was the fact that at its onset members of the Border Ker and Turnbull clans were in the pay-off and fought alongside the English. On seeing that the battle was going against their erstwhile allies they ripped the cross of St George from their armour and fought for their own army.

Ancrum itself is a small village tucked away beside the B6400 with a fine example of a triangular village green complete with thirteenth-century market cross, which is in fact a 'listed building'.

Beyond Lilliardsedge the A68 picks up the line of Dere Street 1½ miles before arriving arriving at St Boswells, named after St Boisil, the first prior of Melrose. Boisil was succeeded by St Cuthbert, who probably began life as a shepherd in the Leader Valley who was in turn called to Lindisfarne to become one of the most revered figures from early British Christianity.

# CHAPTER 6

## *St Boswells to Melrose*

St Boswells has the largest village green in the Borders, the scene of the annual July Boisil's Fair held here since at least the 1600s. Based originally on horse trading where up to 1,000 beasts have been sold in the past the Fair was once the most important event on the Border's scene. James Hogg, The Ettrick Shepherd considered Boisils Fair a more important event than the coronation of George III, turning down an invitation to London, because as a new tenant farmer it would be unseemly if he was not seen at Boisils.

Trading is now a minor consideration at St Boswells Fair and the event is mainly a meeting place for travelling people. The Green is packed for the three-day fair with the elaborate caravans of the travellers, drawn by expensive four-wheel drive vehicles. Palms are still read and fortunes told, a few stalls sell mostly mass-produced goods and James Hogg's 'Vital Fair is now mainly a social event. Perhaps a truer reflection of what the Fair once meant can be found in the St Boswells and District Farmers' Show held on the Saturday following Bosils Fair. Across the road in the Buccleuch Arms a handwritten sign on the door proclaims that for the duration of the Fair these premises will be closed between the hours of 2.30 and 6.00 pm Inside the hotel, to quote a Border saying is, 'gaun like a fair'. Certainly there is no cooking over an open fire for these travellers. Waitresses scurry back and forth serving meals in bar, dining room and lounge, while bar staff strive to keep glasses full.

Locally the 'Saint' at the beginning of the name is dropped. A person will visit 'Boswells' (pronounced 'Boisils') — the local pronunciation truer to the original than the 'proper' version of the name.

A surprise in Newton St Boswells, a mile up the road, is the headquarters of The Borders Regional Council, the body responsible for the regional administration of this vast but lightly populated area. It is no mean task administrating an

145

Fortune teller St Boswells Fair

area stretching from the North Sea to the wilds of Tweedsmuir — from the Cheviots to Soutra Pass — but why choose Newton St Boswells as a base? Diplomacy is the answer, otherwise could it have been Galashiels — Hawick — Selkirk — Kelso — Jedburgh? The selection of any one over the other would have been viewed with suspicion by those unsuccessful in becoming the Regional capital.

North across Tweed from St Boswells, where the river takes a horseshoe loop, stand the ruins of Dryburgh, the only Border Abbey without its surrounding town. Here, on the broad grassy haugh above the river, the setting and the atmosphere of Dryburgh are unique when compared to its contemporaries. Smooth clipped lawns sweep almost to the banks of Tweed. Overhead ancient trees, including Cedars of Lebanon, which may have been brought back from the Crusades along with a reputed eight-hundred-year-old yew, cast a shade enjoyed centuries ago by Dryburgh's pious inhabitants.

While Dryburgh Abbey was founded in 1150 as the first monastic establishment of the White Canons of the

Dryburgh Abbey

Premonstratensian Order in Scotland, the site possibly had earlier religious connections. In the early seventh century Moden, an Irish Culdee saint and follower of St Columba, had his sanctuary here at — Darach Bruach — 'the grove of the oaks'. In earlier times Druids practised an older pagan religion in this same place.

For a period following the invasion of the pagan king of Northumbria the early work of St Moden seems to have been swept aside, leaving it to Saints Aidian, Boisil and Cuthbert to recommence the work of the earlier Columban missionaries.

Despite its present-day rural setting Dryburgh's ruins are less complete than would be expected. Stones from Dryburgh Abbey have been found in excavations of outbuildings attached to Smailholm Tower. Compared to Jedburgh the original abbey building at Dryburgh seems to have been completed in a remarkably short time. The *Chronicle of Melrose* records that by December 1152, 'the monastery was in that place', two short years after founding.

Dryburgh and its abbots never attained the wealth or political influence of the other great Border religious institutions. Written records also seem less prodigious in the day-to-day events surrounding the Abbey and its canons. The Abbot was one of the 104 commissioners nominated when Edward I laid claim to the Scottish crown.

Forces of Edward II left Dryburgh ablaze in 1322, causing severe damage. Andrew, abbot of Dryburgh, with his Border contemporaries was present at Roxburgh in 1355 when Edward Balliol resigned the Scottish kingdom to Edward III. Their compliance in this transaction saved their churches from the fate of others, such as Haddington, destroyed by the English on their subsequent march to Edinburgh to seek the allegiance of Scottish nobility.

Andrew was still Abbot in 1385 when Richard II raided the Borders and left Dryburgh 'devasted by fire'. By the fifteenth century Dryburgh was involved in numerous lawsuits concerning the ownership of its lands, marking an era when monastic life and even the Church itself was falling into disrespect among the populace.

The last abbot died in 1507, and thereafter it became the custom to appoint commendators rather than abbots as heads of religious establishments. In November 1544 Sir George Bowes and Sir Brian Laiton, with 700 men, sacked the town and abbey of Dryburgh. Both were killed at Ancram in February of the following year.

It should not be thought that in the cross-Border forays the English were unique in burning abbey and church. When Scots forces raided the south they were the equal with torch and fire upon houses secular or holy. As the ballad, 'The Battle of Otterburn' recounts:

> Then they hae harried the dales o' Tyne,
> And half o' Bambrough-shire,
> And the Otter-dale they burned it haill,
> And set it a' on fire.

Neither town nor abbey were ever rebuilt. By 1561 Dryburgh was home for one sub-prior and eight canons. In 1584 only two remained, while in 1600 the commendator recorded among other papers 'all the convent thairof being now deceased.'

Scott's View

This is, of course, in the shadow of the Eildon Hills, in Scott Country. Here at Dryburgh is the final resting place of Sir Walter — The Wizard of the North.

But for the actions of a spendthrift grand-uncle the ownership of Dryburgh might have passed to Sir Walter. Because of this grand-uncle's (Robert Haliburton's) incompetence in business the abbey lands purchased by his father Thomas had to be sold. Sir Walter's father had been tempted to and was in a position to buy Dryburgh but was dissuaded from doing so by his own father. Rights of sepulchre were granted to Sir Walter's father and two uncles by the Earl of Buchan in 1791, leading to Sir Walter's comment that, (for the Scott family) 'there was nothing left of Dryburgh but the right of stretching our bones there'.

Scott's death was a cause for national mourning. The press of the day featured black mourning bands when the news was announced. On the day of his burial the waters of Tweed echoed the mood of the people, running heavy and sullen in spate.

From Abbotsford, through Melrose and Darnick Scott's people lined the route. All business ceased, while a black crepe banner of mourning hung from Darnick Tower. So well loved was the poet that his servants petitioned that no hireling should handle his remains between Abbotsford and Dryburgh.

After crossing Leaderfoot bridge the horse-drawn hearse paused at what is now known as 'Scott's View', high above Tweed, across to The Eildons and the compass of the Borderland so loved by Sir Walter. It is said that his own carriage horses, which formed part of the cortege, were so accustomed to stopping here for their master to admire the view, that on this last occasion they did so through force of habit. Two mutes led the procession to St Mary's Aisle in Dryburgh as the press of mourners closed in behind the coffin. Sir Thomas Dick Lauder, who attended the funeral describes the last moments:

> It was not until the harsh sound of the hammers of the workmen who were employed to rivet those iron bars covering the grave to secure it from violation had begun to echo from the vaulted roof that some of us who were called to the full conviction of the fact that the earth had for ever closed over that form which we were wont to love and reverence . . .

A granite block has replaced the iron gratings over Scott's grave, bearing the simple inscription:

Sir Walter Scott, Baronet.
Died September 21, A.D. 1832.

Haigs of Bemerside also hold burial rights at Dryburgh, the most famed of these being Field-Marshal Earl Haig, appointed Commander-in-Chief of the Western Front in 1915. The Haigs are said to be one of the oldest families in the Borders, Douglas Haig being the created Earl in recognition of his war service and the estate of Bemerside purchased from another branch of the Haig family on his behalf by a grateful nation.

Thomas The Rhymer of Ercildoune below the Eildons, to whom are attributed many prophecies, gave a blessing to Haig or Haga of Bemersyde:

Tyde what may betyde,
Haig shall be Haig of Bemersyde.

An undated charter concerning Petrus de Haga's due to the Chapel of St Cuthbert at Old Melrose around the reign of

Alexander II or III was witnessed and signed by Thomas of Ercildoune.

Nearby, overlooking Tweedale, stands a nineteenth-century statue depicting the Scottish hero Wallace. Known as 'The Wallace', stone mason John Smith of Darnick was originally commissioned by Lord Buchan to carve from the huge block of sandstone a monument to Robert Burns. When the somewhat eccentric earl saw the size of the raw block of stone he felt it would be wasted on a man of lesser physical stature, and he decided instead that the figure of Wallace with mighty sword would be a better subject. 'The Wallace' is over 22 feet tall, a grown man reaching just over half way up the round shield bearing the cross of St Andrew held in the statue's left hand. The statue was unveiled by Lord Buchan on 22 September 1814.

Across Tweed from Bemerside on the north bank, Monksford lies midway between here and Dryburgh. Old Melrose was the site of an early monastery of the Celtic Church. Melrose is thought to have been derived from maol-ros, 'the open or naked headland' in the old Celtic tongue. Where Dryburgh sits beside a horseshoe bend of Tweed, at Old Melrose, the river first curves away north-east and swings around the compass points to finish cutting back almost north-west, threatening to rejoin its original course.

Founded by St Aidan sometime in the seventh century, Old Melrose, Mailros or Meuros, had as its first prior, St Boisil. St Cuthbert (of Lindisfarne fame) followed St Boisil as prior until summoned to be Abbot of Lindisfarne in 644. St Cuthbert's calling to the Church is said to have begun when, along with other youths, he was indulging in rough-and-tumble play beside the River Leader. One of his companions, said to be only three years old, admonished Cuthbert for such foolishness, saying, 'Why do you, holy Cuthbert and prelate, give yourself up to these things which are so opposite to your nature and rank? It does not become you to be playing among children when the Lord has appointed you to be a teacher even to those who are older than yourself.' From that day Cuthbert dedicated himself to the work of the Gospel with his special love for animals and birds. Two hundred years later St Cuthbert's body, now interred below the high altar of Durham Cathedral, rested temporarily at

Wallace Statue

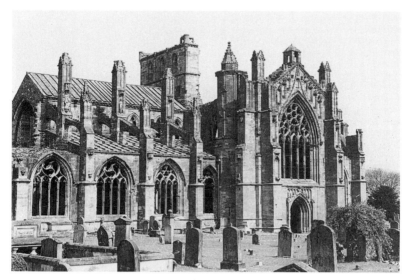

Melrose Abbey

Old Melrose after being removed from Lindisfarne for fear of desecration by raiding Danes.

Despite being destroyed by King Kenneth of Scotland in 839, Old Melrose, the last bastion of the Celtic church in Scotland, continued to be a place of sanctity into the eleventh century, being one of the four main places of pilgrimage in Scotland at the time.

It was under the patronage of King David I that a group of White Monks of the Cistercian Order came north from Rievaulx in Yorkshire to found a new abbey at Old Melrose. The site proved unsuitable for their plans and they selected instead Little Fordell. Melrose, abbey and town, occupy what was once Little Fordell below the Eildons, yet Dorothy Wordsworth expressed to Scott on visiting Old Melrose: 'We wished we could have brought the ruins of Melrose to this spot'.

Founded in 1136 Melrose was the first Cistercian house in Scotland, with the abbey being dedicated, like all Cistercian churches, to The Blessed Virgin in 1146. Original grants of land were for the granges of Eildon, Melrose and Darnick. Royal lands were added from the forests of Selkirk and Traquair,

Picking flowers for preserving Priorswood Gardens Melrose

pasturage of sheep and cattle plus firewood and fishing rights on Tweed.

Melrose seems to have been a particular favourite of David I, as under his patronage the lands held by the Abbey spread through southern Scotland and beyond. From Carrick to Teviotdale lands were held by Melrose, property in Edinburgh, Haddington and Lanark, saltmarsh, Lammermuir grazings all added to the wealth of the Cistercian Order at Melrose.

The wealth of Melrose Abbey must have caused some envy among the powerful landowners of the Borders:

> The monks of Melrose made fat kail
> On Fridays, when they fasted;
> But wanted neither beef nor ale,
> As long's their neighbour's lasted.

– meaning that all in all the monks had an easy life compared to that of the surrounding populace.

Richard the first Abbot remained in office for only two years. Despite his being reputedly a pious learned monk his quick temper led to his removal in 1148. Waldeve, his successor, refused all offers of promotion, remaining at Melrose until his death in 1159. Waldeve's tomb became a place of pilgrimage where miracles were performed, and proof of his sanctity was noted twelve years later when his body and clothing were found to be intact when his tomb was opened.

This story must have been known to Scott, when, in the, *Lay of the Last Minstrel*, William of Deloraine and the Monk of St Mary's aisle raised the slab covering the tomb of the. Wizard Michael Scott:

> Before their eyes the Wizard lay,
> As if he had not been dead a day,
> His hoary beard in silver rolled,
> He seemed some seventy winters old;
> A palmer's amice wrapped him round,
> With a wrought Spanish baldric bound,
> Like a pilgrim from beyond the sea,
> His left hand held his Book of Might;
> A silver cross was in his right;
> The lamp was placed beside his knee;
> High and majestic was his look,
> At which the fellest fiends had shook,
> And all unruffled was his face:
> They trusted his soul had gotten grace.

An eerie scene indeed, enough to frighten even such a doughty warrior as Deloraine. The priest dare not even look upon the dead wizard, but prayed with eyes averted from the tomb, urging Deloraine to hasten:

> Now speed thee what thou hast to do,
> Or, Warrior, we may dearly rue;
> For those, thou mayst not look upon,
> Are gathering fast round the yawning stone!

Then Deloraine, in terror, took
From the cold hand the Mighty Book,
With iron clasped and with iron bound:

He thought, as he took it, the dead man frowned;
But the glare of the sepulchral light,
Perchance had dazzled the Warrior's sight.

The grave is closed with accompanying unworldy voices, sobs and laughter. Deloraine sped back to Branksome with the vital book of spells; by noon the next day the monk was dead.

Scottish kings seem to have had a liking for Melrose Abbey. King Alexander was, according to his wishes, buried there after dying on the island of Kerrera near Oban in 1249. Unable to crusade to the Holy Land himself, King Robert Bruce on his death bed requested his friend James Douglas to carry his heart before him to Palestine. After his death Bruce's heart was removed to be carried forward by Douglas in a desperate charge against the Saracens.

Sir James, it is said, flung the casket forward to encourage his men in the attack. The Douglas was found slain, his body covering the casket which was returned for burial, as Bruce requested, at Melrose. In 1921 a lead casket containing a mummified heart was found during the course of excavations, but there is no proof as to whether or not this belonged to King Robert Bruce.

During the later part of Robert Bruce's reign Melrose enjoyed a degree of prosperity as the monks diversed into the wool trade, among other things. A retaliatory raid by Richard II following a Scots incursion south left Melrose in ashes. The abbey ruins as seen today are the result of rebuilding from this period.

Notable Abbots of Melrose, such as Andrew Hunter, King's Treasurer in 1450, became inclined to leave the running of the religious life to their priors, involving themselves more and more as advisers and statemen to the monarchy.

Gradually the wealth of Churches such as Melrose began to attract secular interests, as kings appointed laymen or their own sons as commendators, mainly it appears to collect for their own interests the dues payable to the abbeys. James V in 1532 successfully petitioned Pope Clement VII on behalf of his eldest natural son, James Stewart, whose appointment was confirmed in 1541.

The year 1544 saw the large-scale destruction by Sir Ralph Evers of town and abbey. The abbey church was burned and the Douglas tombs were desecrated. Decline set in because the commendator was more interested in securing funds for his own purse rather than effecting repairs upon the building.

Things had reached a sorry state when, in 1556, the sub-prior and three monks complained that the commendator had sold to the Bishop of Glasgow the sheet lead urgently needed to make the church and their quarters watertight. A further complaint from the same year alleged that the commendator had refused to admit new brethren to the Order. This meant that not only was it approaching the stage when there were insufficient monks to conduct services but equally the protection of their property was becoming equally difficult.

By 1573 we find Sir Walter Scott of Branxholm removing from the choir numerous fittings, stones, lead and iron for the purpose of 'protecting them from the English raiders'. Jo Watson, who seems to have been the last monk, died in 1590, and with him the sanctified life of Melrose Abbey, which, if the earlier settlement of the Celtic church is taken into account, spanned a period of a thousand years.

In 1618 a parish church was constructed within the former monks' choir where worship continued for two centuries. Despite the ravages of years and reformers the ruin of Melrose Abbey can still boast some fine stonework, including intricate and unusual statues. Many carvings were defaced during the height of covenanting zeal in the mid-seventeenth century. The despoiler of the Virgin and Child is related to have had his arm permanently disabled when the head of the infant Christ fell on his arm.

Before leaving Melrose, the last of the Border Abbeys on our tour, we should cast our minds back to the effect these buildings had upon the surrounding populace. Although during their lifetime the abbeys were much improved and even rebuilt, even in their original form they must have been in stark contrast to the dwellings of the ordinary people.

Castle and tower of the nobility were crude in comparison to the intricate stonework wrought by imported masons. It must have been with a sense of awe that the farm labourer, the herdsman and the tradesman saw these buildings rise in unaccustomed intricate splendour.

Little is known of the masons who wrought the columns and bosses these many centuries ago other than their 'masons mark' identifying their work. One left more than his simple trademark at Melrose Abbey. John Morow gave a blessing to the building on a plaque now removed to the museum in the commendator's house and replaced by a replica:

'John Maro: Sum Tyme: Callit:
Was: I: And Born: In: Parysee:
Certainly: And Had: In: Kepping:
All: Mason: Work: Of: Santan:
Druys: Ye: Hye: Kyrk: Of Glasgu:
Melros: and: Pasley: Of:
Nyddysdayll: And: Of Galway:
I: Pray: To: God: And: Mary: Baith:
And: Sweet: St: John: Keep: This: Haly:
Kirk: Fraw: Skaith:

Marrow could have been the first Master of the St John's Lodge of Freemasons in Scotland; nearby Newstead has the oldest Masonic Lodge in Scotland; the Festival of St John is celebrated at Melrose each year on December 27th.

Where once the monks of Melrose cultivated their crops can now be found Priorwood Gardens, a property of the National Trust for Scotland. Alongside is the Trust shop and a Tourist Information Centre. Local members of the Trust tend Priorwood Gardens where the speciality is flowers suitable for drying, and the techniques for this art. Inside the drying and display room the air is heady — almost intoxication with the sent of potpourri petals and flowers being prepared for display.

Attached is Priorwood Orchard which tells the story of 'Apples thro' the Ages', which began in Roman times with the introduction of cultivated fruit to replace the hard sour native scrogs or wild apple. The orchard forms a cool calm haven below the trees — plenty of picnic tables — while just over the wall the daily bustle of Melrose at the height of the summer season passes by unseen and scarcely heard.

Melrose Abbey is still the scene of some celebration when, during the Melrose Festival, the Festival Queen, the Dux Girl of Melrose Grammar School, is crowned within the ruins by the wife of the guest speaker of the day. Melrose Festival is led by The Melrosian, a bachelor supported by his right and left-hand men, the two previous Melrosians.

The rideout takes place on the Monday evening, encompassing the Eildons, a crossing of the Tweed, and a visit to Newstead, which not only claims to possess the senior Masonic Lodge but also to be the oldest inhabited village in Scotland. One of the final events for the Melrose Festival is the 'Eildon hill Race'. This is now included in the British Fell Running Championships, in which some of Britain's best participants in this punishing sport now compete.

While in Melrose a look at the Eildon Hills may be appropriate, as most writers this one included cite this Border town as, 'lying in the shadow of the Eildons.' The Melrose song describes the towns situation with perfection:

> By Tweed's flashing rill 'neath the Eildon Hill,
> There is set a jewel fair,
> Tho' we wander far o'er the wide wide world,
> Oor hearts still linger there.

Formed of volcanic rock 300 million years ago The Eildons were never hills in their own right. The molten rock pushing upwards from the earth's core failed to penetrate the layers of existing sedimentary material. An active volcano did exist between Mid Hill and Wester Hill at Little Hill, spewing out ash and rubble, but contributed nothing to the Eildons as we know them today.

Weathering, with no little assistance from the ice sheet which covered the Borders 100,000 years ago, eroded and scraped away overlaying sedimentary rocks and rubble, leaving the triple peaks standing bold against the surrounding country.

The Iron Age Selegovae tribe established a major base on North Hill, one of the largest hill forts in Southern Scotland. Within the triple wall twenty-acre site there are some 296 hut circles. Along came the Romans bent on further conquest to further the glory that was Rome. Perhaps the invaders evicted

Trimontium Monument in the shadow of the Eildons

the Selegovae from their North Hill camp, where they sited a signal station, or after a period of conflict Roman and Celt shared the summit. Below lay Newstead, or as the Romans knew it, Trimontium, named after the three peaks of the Eildons. This was the most important Roman outpost in ancient Caledon where the Roman commander could within twenty-four hours direct troops to any trouble-spot in the Tweed basin. Designed for a thousand troops there sprung up around the fort three annexes where there took place extensive iron working, pottery, glass and brickmaking.

Some of the most outstanding finds relating to the Roman occupation of Scotland have been found at Trimontium in pits which could have been wells serving iron workers' forges. Many of the principal artifacts, such as ceremonial helmets from these pits, were made between 1905 and 1910, when a Melrose solicitor, Dr James Curle, and the Society of Antiquaries of Scotland, conducted the first investigations on the site.

'The Newstead Project' is currently under way funded by a number of national and local bodies under the direction of Dr Dick Jones of Bradford University's Department of Archaeological Sciences. Modern techniques, such as a magnetometer survey revealing the iron works and other non-destructive methods of archaelogical science, are being employed in this modern dig. This study is to extend beyond the life of the Romans in the Borders and will examine a number of sites for evidence of the newcomers' influence upon the native tribes of the area.

Artifacts from excavations at Trimontium are displayed within the Commendator's House at Melrose Abbey and in National Museums. Established in 1991 is a more a permanent exhibition of Trimontium in Melrose Corn Exchange — 'Trimontium — A Roman Frontier Post and its People'. Organised by 'The Trimontium Trust' under chairman Walter Elliot, the exhibition makes a more fitting display for this very important Roman site in Scotland.

Walter Elliot's interest in the Trimontium site extends back through his working life spent in forestry and fencing work. Walking the Trimontium site when clear of crops Walter began to realise that here was not only a Roman Fort, but as iron slag, broken bricks and glass shards were being seen on the surface here was also a site with an industrial past. For years Walter Elliot's attempts to interest museums and archaeologists in this extra dimension of Trimontium met with frustration.

While the ability to fell a tree where required or erect a taut stock-proof wire fence are essential skills in Border rural life, with learned societies they cut little ice where the study of Roman History is concerned. Fortunately Walter Elliot persisted with the present Trimontium exhibition, set to run initially for five years, and largely result of his efforts. For Walter it has been the culmination of a lifetime's ambition to see the establishment of a permanent museum to the Roman Occupation established in Scotland, especially when such august books as *History of the English Speaking Peoples* cite the Trimontium mask as, 'found at Newstead on Hadrian's Wall'. Where better for such a display than near Trimontium, the principal Roman fort and industrial base in the Borders.

Around the Eildons are a number of walks well within the ability of anyone who is moderately fit, without needing to be a hairy-faced load burdened hillwalker. North Hill 1323 with its fort has a track leading to the top. Walks, by the way, start in Melrose Square, up Dingleton Road for 200 yards where the first waymarker is found.

Mid-Hill is steepest but offers the best views, crowned with an O. S. triangulation pillar at 1,385 feet. It also has a viewpoint indicator dedicated to the memory of Sir Walter Scott. Wester Hill is a dawdle at 1,216 ft but has the most diverse vegetation, including natural regenerated Scots Pine.

A programme of ranger-led walks takes place to the Eildons throughout the summer, including one which discusses the real and the fanciful origins of the Eildons, 'Magma or Magic', and a 'Midsummer's Night Dream' on the night of June 21st.

As if this were not enough for a small town such as Melrose, there is an excellent Motor Museum, signposted near the Abbey available for those who wish to drool over 'real cars' with running boards and separate headlamps.

To rugby enthusiasts, Melrose Rugby Club who play at Greenyards, are known not only for the playing ability of their team, but as the founders of the fast-moving game of seven aside rugby, 'The Melrose Sevens' was the first such contest.

# CHAPTER 7

## *Lauderdale*

When included in the old county of Berwickshire, Lauderdale, the valley of the River Leader, was very much on the fringes of that county. Even for this book it raises some problems, as one of the best-known Border ballads links Thomas Learmont, or Thomas the Rhymer of Ecrildoune, an old tower at Earlston beside the River Leader, with the Eildon Hills near Melrose.

At least three versions of the Rhymer ballad are said to have existed — at Cambridge, Lincoln cathedral and the British Museum. This latter version appears to have been the source used by Sir Walter Scott in his 'Minstrelsy of The Scottish Border.'

Behind a petrol-filling station at Earlston stands the ruin of the Rhymer's Tower. A few paltry feet square it would be hard to imagine that space could have ever have been found within for a family home. A stone tablet on the south-facing wall records that this is 'The Tower of Thomas the Rhymer with Cottage adjoining the property of the Edinburgh Borders County Association 1894'. A quotation is added from Scott's version of the last glimpses of Thomas:

> Farewell my father's ancient tower,
> A long farewell said he,
> The scene of pleasure pomp and power,
> Thou never mair shall see.

Thomas Learmont must have died sometime after 1299, as in that year he granted in a charter the small tower of Ecrildoune to the Trinity of Soltra. Even as late as the nineteenth century when writers such as Scott were collecting these ballads the country people still held in high esteem the poetry and prophesies of The Rhymer.

Some sources say that Thomas was not a prophet but committed to rhyme the utterances of Eliza a nun at Haddington. The questions of who was the soothsayer, whether the words were later used to fit events, or whether they were later forgeries, has been a matter of much learned research and discussion down the centuries. Among other things Thomas is said to have foretold the Battle of Bannockburn: 'The burn of bried shall run fow reid', and the Union of the Crowns: 'When Tweed and Pausayl join at Merlin's grave, Scotland and England shall one monarch have'. There are others, including events as dramatic as the death of King Alexander on the cliffs of Fife, to more mundane matters like a bridge over the Tweed at Leaderfoot: 'At Eildon Tree if you will be, a brigg ower Tweed you there may see'. Yet Thomas was a real person even if the legend associated with his disappearance for seven years can to our modern eyes be discounted as a fairy tale.

Thomas in the ballad, 'Thomas the Rhymer' is kidnapped, highjacked, call it what you want, from beneath the Eildon Tree into seven years' service to the Queen of Elfdom. Thomas it appears was a willing victim if the description of that lady is to be believed, bearing in mind that the fairies and elves of legend have nothing to do with pretty little things flitting on gauze wings or sitting on toadstools. Rather they were in the dim and distant past believed by the populace to be a subterranean dwelling race, a belief held throughout much of northern Europe. Certainly to many people fairies were real and feared. True, Thomas had been lying at his easy on Huntlie Bank below the Eildons when the apparition came upon him dressed in green silk and velvet; even her horse had fifty silver bells hung from its mane:

> True Thomas he pull'd off his cap,
> And louted low down to his knee,
> 'All hail, thou mighty Queen of Heaven!
> For thy peer on earth I never did see.'

William Aytoun gives this version in *The Ballads of Scotland* as 'True Thomas', his other version 'Thomas of Ecrildoune' describes the lady approaching, her dapple grey palfrey bearing a saddle of pure ivory with trappings of gold set with precious stones:

> Thomas rathely up he raise,
> And he ran over that mountain hye,
> And soothly as the story goes,
> He met her by the Eildon Tree.

> He kneeled down upon his knee,
> Underneath the greenwood spray,
> And said, 'Lovely lady, reive, [have pity] on me,
> Queen of heaven, as thou well may!'

Mounted behind the Queen the pair set out for the other world, crossing deserts, passing the ways to wickedness and to righteousness before reaching the road to Elfland. Through rivers of blood, into a garden where she presents Thomas with an apple for wages, which gives him a tongue which can never lie.

> 'Take this for thy wages, True Thomas;
> It will give thee the tongue that will never lie.'

– a gift which in real life is not going to be an asset to Thomas in his every day dealings!

> 'My tongue is my ain!' True Thomas, he said,
> 'A gudley gift ye wad gie tae me!
> I neither docht to buy nor sell,
> At fair or tryste where I may be.'

Thomas is returned to below the Eildon tree after seven years, at the end of the traditional version, while Scott added two further cantos to the tale, the second concerning the Rhymer's prophecies, the third his recall to elfdom, led by a hart and hind parading near his home, which he follows, never to be seen again.

A fairytale indeed — a theme taken up in other Border ballads such as Tamlane. What proves to be intriguing about The Rhymer is where was he for those seven years when he vanished from the sight of his fellow men of Lauderdale? A stone at Earlston Church records, 'auld rhymer race, lived in this place', while Nigel Tranter has based his historical novel *True Thomas* on The Rhymer, taking him off first in elopement, then in royal service for seven years.

The story of True Thomas is not the only one to be associated with the Eildons. Below them sleep the knights of King Arthur ready to spring into action when called to the Nation's aid. Of course the three peaks were originaly one, cleft in three by the

wizard Michael Scott — like The Rhymer a man of flesh and
blood who is recorded in history but credited with magical
powers.

Where Thomas predicted a bridge across the Tweed at
Leaderfoot there are now three — the redundant one and the
new road bridge carrying the A68 up Lauderdale. Upstream
stands the equally redundant rail bridge where no train has
run since the 1960s but one of the best examples of Victorian
engineering to be found anywhere. Only saved from the
demolishers at the last moment the bridge has since had
special status and is subject to further development as a
tourist attraction.

To the west of Lauderdale the Southern Upland Way follows
a parallel track over the high ground from Melrose to Lauder
by way of Kedslie Hill and the Covenanters' Well. The modern
A68 road by Leader side follows an ancient route. A section
of Roman Dere Street is shown high on Dun Law above their
camp at Kirktonhill, although its line through Lauderdale is
uncertain.

Prior to the new local government scheme of the mid-1970s
Lauder enjoyed burgh status; it was the only Royal and Ancient
Burgh in Berwickshire and it now forms part of Ettrick and
Lauderdale District. Lauder's Royal status dates from at least
1502 in a charter from King James IV.

The old tollbooth is said to have stood in the centre of Lauder
since the fourteenth century and it has been rebuilt more than
once, allegedly following the original style. Lauder High Street
has some fine examples of ordinary town-house architecture,
especially the several houses of narrow whinstones set with red
sandstone facings.

Behind the High Street the back lanes, with yards and stables,
show a town layout which must be little changed through the
ages. Skirted by the Southern Upland Way for the pedestrian
at least it is easy to escape from the hustle of the A68 which
passes through the town centre.

Lauder may not be the largest town to uphold Common
Riding celebrations, but it can certainly claim to have one of
the oldest traditions, although the actual boundary riding was
discontinued for a seventy-year period, to be resuscitated in
1911 to celebrate the Coronation of King George V. Unlike the

Lauder Common Riding, the cavalcade setting out

other mounted festivals already mentioned in this book, Lauder Common Riding dates back to when the town's Common Land was marked out with a series of cairns.

When communities were largely self-supporting, the Common lands of burghs such as Lauder played an important part in sustenance living which only totally disappeared this century. Only burgesses had these Rights of Common which at Lauder allowed each burgess to graze 25 sheep and a cow on the burgh's 1,700 acres of Lauder Hill. From a modern viewpoint the heather moorland, peat and scrub may appear of little consequence, but in their time Rights of Common were a zealously guarded privilege.

Qualification as a burgess meant the owning of a 'burgess acre' within the town of which there were originally 105. Originally Common Riding was not a ceremonial occasion but an essential duty to keep cairns and boundary marks in repair and to check if any encroachment had been made on the Common by neighbouring landlords.

In modern terms Lauder Common Riding is just what it says, a confirming and symbolic marking of the old Common boundary where the Cornet places a stone on the only remaining burgess cairn. It is also a cause for local celebration. Following a week of events, including what is claimed to be the best fancy-dress parade in the Borders, the first Saturday in August marks Lauder Common Riding proper.

The Cornet, as the principal in Lauder's Common Riding is called, must have a residential qualification within Lauderdale, and must have participated in the event on at least one previous occasion. Support comes from the right and left hand men, from the Cornets of the two previous years and of course from the Cornet's Lass. Over 300 riders make up the cavalcade on a range of mounts from the smartly turned out horses owned by the principles, those hired for the occasion and, perhaps the most appropriate for the Common, shaggy farm horses such as would have been ridden when the event was for real.

It's an early start for Common Riding day. To the first time visitor it comes as a surprise to find all the pubs open with the crowd overspilling into the street at 7.00 am. Through traffic is diverted away from the town by a convenient loop on the A697. The roar of passing vehicles is replaced for at least one day by the clatter of iron-shod hooves as the cavalcade assembles behind the Tollbooth.

The stage is set, with dignitaries gathered on the Tollbooth steps, where the first herald of the occasion is the strains of, 'Bonnie Lauderdale':

> Lauderdale! Bonnie Lauderdale,
> Sae dear tae me,
> I will sing in praise where'erI go,
> O'Bonnie Lauderdale.

Scottish Brewers' Silver Band from Newtongrange lead the Cornet forward to receive the town banner with the promise to return it unsullied and untarnished following the boundary riding. The brief ceremony over, the Cornet re-mounts to lead the cavalcade around the streets of Lauder before heading for the Waterin' Stane beside the Lauder-Stow road.

Here refreshments are served to the riders and toasts drunk to, 'The Queen', 'The Cornet' and 'The Chairman'. Amber liquid is diluted with ice-cold spring-fed hill water flowing into

Filling water for refreshments at 'Waterin Stane' Lauder Common Riding

a roadside trough. Water which is considered by at least one Lauder resident to be superior to that from any other source for adding to the national drink. Bottles filled at the Waterin' Stane are an essential part of his luggage when embarking to distant rugby matches in far-flung less civilised corners of Britain.

Horses other than those of the Cornet and his immediate supporters are kept at a distance, where juvenile horse holders may earn a shilling or two while the riders mingle with the crowd below. In the small layby only official cars can be accommodated; other car followers must walk five hundred yards or so to hear the toasts and a verse of 'Jeanie's Black E'e' sung by a choir of ex-Cornets beside the Waterin' Stane. Refreshed the riders continue to the Burgess Cairn then back to Lauder for a ceremony at the War Memorial and the conclusion of handing back the town flag.

Lauder Common Riding begins officially on the preceding Sunday with the Kirking of The Cornet Service in the Parish Church. Dating from 1673 in the form of a Greek cross with central tower the present Lauder Kirk is said to have atrocious acoustics. In an earlier building a bunch of gung-ho Scottish nobles administered a piece of mid-fifteenth century 'instant' and 'final' justice.

James III held the throne of Scotland at the time, his father James II having been killed by the exploding cannon at the siege of Roxburgh while the former was but a child. Unlike his predecessor, James III was not inclined to warlike pursuits, preferring instead the gentle company of artists, musicians and architects.

This was a major upset of the *status quo* where the Scottish earls and barons were concerned, since they invariably expected to be prominent in the affairs of court and close to the king in all matters concerning the state. Slowly the pot of resentment seethed and bubbled before finally boiling over at Lauder, where, in 1482, an army of Scots was assembled for yet another dispute with an English king, in this instance Edward IV.

There were more pressing matters for the Scottish lords to deal with before advancing any further south. This was the problem of Cochrane, Rogers, Leonard, Hommel and Torphichen — the kings favourites. Ensconced in Lauder Church the nobles proposed and counter-proposed, debated

and better debated the course of action which most of the
company desired but were reluctant to put into direct words.
This was the simple proposal of how to murder the King's
friends and get away with it.

One, Lord Gray, brought their attention to the fable of the
mice who lived in daily fear of being captured and eaten by a
quiet-treading pussy footed cat. A council of mice was held, not
unlike that upon which they themselves were embarked upon,
Lord Gray pointed out how the mice would find a solution to
their problem.

Their safest bet, the mouse council in their debate decided,
was that the placing of a bell around the cat's neck would
give an ample early warning of the approach of puss. 'But',
said Lord Gray, 'who would bell the cat?' — a somewhat high
risk undertaking. There was one among the cautious assembly,
Archibald Douglas, Early of Angus. 'I am he,' said the bold
earl, 'who will bell the cat,'. Just then a clamorous banging on
the door announced Cochrane, the most hated of the King's
companions, demanding to know the purpose of the meeting
and to be admitted.

Dressed in the best of gear, Cochrane far outshone the
nobles, who would not exactly have been wearing the hodden
grey of the common populace. Silks and velvets, with many
a tassel and other trimmings, formed his attire, set off by
a fine wrought gold chain around his neck. Among further
accessories was a gold-tipped hunting bugle at his belt. His
helmet, carried before him, was inlaid with precious metals,
and it was rumoured that his tent ropes were of fine silk rather
than the common course hemp.

Archibald Douglas met Cochrane in the aisle pulling the gold
chain from off his neck saying, 'A halter would better become
him.' Robert Douglas snatched the bugle, saying, 'Thou hast
been a hunter of mischief too long.' Cochrane, poor chap, who
had never met the ilk of these gentry before, actually asked,
'Is this jest or earnest, my lords?' Of course it was the latter;
there was nothing more dangerous than a noble who thought
his nose pushed out of joint in 1482. Soon Cochrane's friends
were also captured and quickly tried for having misled the King
and misgoverned the nation. Guilty, of course, the unfortunate
men were hung from Lauder bridge.

Thirlestane Castle [the name denotes a mill], one of several places in the Borders to bear this name, stands amid parklands downstream of Lauder. It is the possible scene of the ballad 'Auld Maitland'. This was considered by Scott to be a poem of great antiquity which he had collected from the mother of James Hogg, The Ettrick Shepherd, who sang or chanted the ballad with great animation.

'Auld Maitland' begins with the siege of a 'darksome house' in 'Leader-Town' by a force led by one described as a nephew of King Edward of southern land.

> 'Wha hauds this house?' young Edward cry'd,
> 'Or wha gies't it ower tae me?'
> A gray-hair'd knight set up his head,
> And crackit right crousely:
> 'Of Scotland's King I haud my house;
> He pays me meat and fee;
> And I will keep my guid auld house,
> While my house will keep me.'

Auld Maitland repulsed the fifteen-day siege with a mixture of defensive ploys, such as burning tar barrels and muckle stanes, sending the young Edward home with a flea in his ear plus fifteen boatloads of plunder from the Merse and Teviotdale.

The scene shifts to France:

> Then they are on to the land o' France,
> Where auld King Edward lay,
> Burning baith castle, tower and town,
> That he met on his way.

Auld Maitland's three sons were in France, 'Learning at school alas!' On seeing the arms of Scotland quartered with King Edward they conclude that Scotland has been conquered. The three of them become involved in the local politics of fire and sword, having the audacity to pose as sons of a northern English noble to steal King Edward's standard.

Pursuit ensues, but the three Maitlands get refuge in one of the besieged towns or castles, darting out and in to slay so many of their enemy that carts and wains were yoked to haul the victims away. Three of King Edward's champions and the young Edward meet the same fate: little wonder that Mrs Hogg gave the ballad over with some excitement.

Thirlestane's original defensive tower dates from the 13th century. An extensive rebuilding operation in the 16th, followed over the centuries by additions and improvements, made it a suitable seat for the earls, and for the one and only Duke of Lauderdale. It is the home of descendants of the Maitland family to this day.

Originally the second Earl or Duke had been a supporter of the Covenant, but later changed sides to the Royalist faction. Exiled with Charles II he returned to be captured at the battle of Worcester, his head being saved from the block only by the Restoration.

Following the Restoration the Duke, through his previous support of Charles, became virtually ruler of Scotland on the King's behalf. As can often happen with absolute power the Duke became corrupt and seeking to further his own interests rather than those of the state or people, leading to a rift between him and the Establishment.

Sometimes the incident of the snowball in June, prior to the dukedom, is held up as a redeeming factor in the later character of the Duke, or perhaps he was involved in a piece of cat and mouse play, never thinking he could lose. Following a bitter winter, Tam and Maggie Hardie, tenants of Midside, were unable to pay their rent. Maggie went to the second Earl with her tale of severe weather and no money. 'Well', he said, 'if the weather has been as bad as you say a snow ball in June will serve in lieu of rent.'

Snow on the Lammermuirs in June is a rarity, yet Maggie Hardie, by packing a shaded crevice and then covering it with turf, was able to deliver the required payment. When the Duke was exiled and then imprisoned the Hardies saved the rent due from them and eventually they baked the coins inside a bannock delivered by her to the noble at the Tower. This clandestine payment, it is said, was instrumental in saving the Earl's life. On regaining his freedom he gave Maggie and her children their farm rent-free for life.

Part of Thirlestane is open to the public, including state rooms, the family nurseries, with a wide display of childrens toys over the ages, and the old domestic apartments, where some of the drudgery of past generations of servants can well be imagined.

Featured here are also the Border Country Life Exhibitions with a wide display of life down through he ages in the Borders' agricultural community. The interior of an entire tailor's shop can be seen as it was when the last country craftsman finally laid down his needle in the village of Allanton in Berwickshire. While at Thirlestane keep an eye open for the ghost of the Duke of Lauderdale said to haunt the castle.

A number of local events are held annually in Thirlestane grounds, including Horse Trials and the two day Scottish Championships took place there in August 1991.

Here, where the open vale of the Leader sweeps down from the Lammermuirs and the Lothian watershed, we must leave this part of the Borders Region, town and village, kirk and abbey, castle and cottage, which have seen so much of Scottish history. Westward lie the milltowns, the riever country of Teviot and Liddle, the ballads of Ettrick and Yarrow and the rich heritage of Peeblesshire — all part of another story — the subject of *Discovering the Borders II*.

# Further Reading List

*The Verge of Scotland*: W. T. Palmer: Robert Hale, London
*The Scottish Border and Northumberland*: John T. White: Eyre Methuen, London
*The Rivers of Scotland*: Dick Lauder: T Morison, Glasgow
*Tales of a Grandfather*: Scott
*Coldingham Priory and Parish*: A. Thomson F.S.A.: Graighead Bros, Galashiels
*The Poetical Works of Sir Walter Scott*: Scott
*The Scott Country*: Crockett: A & C Black, London
*Companion to Tweed*: G. Burnett: Methuen and Co, London
*The Steel Bonnets*: G. M. Fraser: Barrie & Jenkins, London
*Gold at Wolfs Craig*: Fred Douglas
*Fast Castle: Mitchell*: Edinburgh Archaeological Society
*Kelsae*: Alistair Moffat: Mainstream, Edinburgh
*The Proceedings of the Berwickshire Naturalists Club*
Various publications of the Scottish Borders Tourist Board and the Borders Regional Council.

# Index

Abbey St Bathans 13, 75–76
Accent Borders 20–21
Aitken-Walker Louise 89
Ancrum Moor 4, 143
Ayton Castle 59, 99

Berwick Barracks 110–112
Berwick Bridges 108–110
Berwick on Tweed name origin 103
Berwick Borough 103–105
Berwick Eliz. Walls 106–107
Berwick Rangers 115–116
Berwickshire 3, 5, 6
Birgham Treaty of 60
Borders Region 5
Borders Regional Council 11
Burrel Sir William 112
Burnmouth 54

Carter Bar 7, 132
Carham 7, 60
Cessford Castle 124
Cheviot 7
Chew Green 132
Chirnside 79
Clark Jim 87–89
Coldingham, Priory, village 40–42
Coldstream, abbey, bridge, marriage
  house, Guards, festival 93–97
Cockburnspath, Copath,
  Coldbranspaith 25–26
Common Ridings 21
Cove Harbour 26–29
Crumstane Farm Park 90–91
Cumledge Mill 78

David 1st King 3, 11
D'Arcy 91
Dere Street 131
Dryburgh Abbey 6, 146–50
Dunglass Collegiate Church 25
Duns 83–89
Duns Castle, Nature Reserve
  84–86
Duns Scotus 83–84

Earlston 6
Eccles 4
Edins Broch 77
Eildon Hills 6, 149–50, 159–162
Erskine Henry 79
Evers or Eures 4, 143
Eyemouth, town, harbour, fishing
  industry, East Coast Disaster,
  festival, lifeboat rescue, salmon
  fishing, smuggling 43–52
Eye river 12
Education 24

Fast Castle 32–34
Ferniehirst Castle 140
Flodden Battle 8, 94, 95
Flood 1948 12–14
Floors Castle 125–126
Fogo 80
Foulden 80–81

Golf, local courses 20
Gordon 72
Greenlaw, Grinly 67–68
Greenknowe Tower 72
Geology 8, 9, 31, 60

Halidon Hill battle 8, 100, 103
Heriots Dyke 72
Hirsel (Douglas Homes) 97–99
Home family 5, 65–66
Home David of Wedderburn 91
Home Grisel 69–72
Hume Castle 65–67
Hume David 79
Hutton Castle 112

James IV 55
James VI 3
Jedburgh, Jeddart, Jethart 132–140
Jedburgh Abbey 136–138
John Wood Collection 41, 42

Kelso, Kelsae name origin 117
Kelso Square 117

Kelso Show 118–119
Kelso Abbey 122
Ker family Dukes of Roxburghe 5,
    124–125
Kirkwood Archie 6

Lamberton, Toll, Kirk 54–55
Lammermuir Hills 12
Lauder 166–170
Lauder Common Riding 166–170
Lauderdale 6
Lauder Kirk 170–171
Layton or Laiton 4, 143
Leges Marchairum 5
Lilliards Edge *see* Ancrum Moor
Linton 1, 131
Longformacus 75

Manderston House 89–90
March as border 4, 5
Marchmont House 68–69
Mellerstain House 70–72
Mersington 4
Merse The meaning and situation
    56–57, 60
Melrose Abbey 153–159
Melrose festivals 159
Monteviot Woodland Centre
    140–141
Mutiny Stones 75

Nisbet 4
Newtown St Boswells 5, 146
Newstead Project 160–161

Old Melrose, Mailros, Meuros 151,
    153
Ottandi 2

Pease Dene 30
Peniel Heugh 141
Pennine Way 7
Pollard 4
Polworth, Pollart, kirk & legend
    69–70
Priorwood Gardens 158

Queen Mary's House 136, 139

Radio local 23–24
Redheugh 31–32
Redeswire, raid 132–135
Roads description 22–23
Roxburgh Castle/burgh 123–124

St Abbs, Head, lighthouse, village,
    nature reserve 35–39
St Boswells, Boisils 144
St Boisil 151
St Cuthbert 151, 153
St Ebbe 35–36
Saint Helens on the lea 31
Scott Walter at Kelso and
    Sandyknowe 127–129
Scottish Borders Enterprise 11
Salmon Netting 81–82, 113–114
Salmon Poaching 114–115
Selegovae 2
Siccar Point 31
Small James 64
Spittal 105–106
Steel David 6
Swinton, family, kirk, village 99–102

Television Local 24
Thirlstane Castle 172–174
Thomas the Rhymer 150, 163–166
Trimontium 160–161
Tweed Acts 16
Tweed Angling 16–18
Tweedmouth 105
Twinlaw Cairns, legend 72

Wallace Statue 151
Wark 8
Watch Water 75
Westruther 72
Wedderburn Castle 59, 99
Wellington Monument *see* Peniel
    Heugh

Yetholm 2, 129–131